Body as Teacher

Yoga's Physical Practices for All

Part II of the Fusion Yoga method

By Charmion O'Day Harris

*This book is dedicated to the many students and teachers
that inspire me and countless others with your wisdom, openness, and inner strength.
Thank you for sharing this path.*

Living True Works
3710 Farnum Creek Rd
Milford, KS 66514
www.wildsukha.com

Library of Congress Cataloging-in-Publication-Data
Body as Teacher: Yoga's Physical Practices for All
ISBN: 979-8-9940836-3-5

Other Living True Works:

The Guru is You: Yoga for Self-Discovery and Purposeful Living is a companion book that fuses yogic philosophy, history, and culture, the 8 Limbs, Chakra and Enneagram systems, the Gita, Ayurvedic practices, deep inner work, fusion sequencing and teaching methodology, business principles, and story-telling as part of your map of unique evolution. *The Guru is You* and *Body as Teacher* together comprise the Fusion Yoga Method.

Backstory

My childhood in the Midwest was grounded by a hard-working mostly single mother and the parameters of the Catholic church. It was equally wilded by my cowboy father with no parameters except reliance on oneself. So, at eighteen years old, the Army seemed like a good fit for me – and it was. I became tougher than I had dreamed possible. But my new outer fortitude brought with it a new inner numbness.

After a few years, motherhood and college softened my edges. But still, something remained amiss between my head, heart, and body. So, the kids and I headed for the last frontier where I laid my problem on Mother Nature's alter by hiking straight up mountains and steering directly into the sea. Suddenly, tidal waves of emotion met me every day and most nights. It worked; my dam had broken. But I didn't yet have the tools to embrace both grit and vulnerability, so I set out again searching for wholeness through adventures that put survival to the test. This time my body wasn't as forgiving.

When I could no longer override or outrun myself, I turned to yoga. Soon thereafter, in a small studio in California, I experienced awareness beyond my wildest dreams. What I'd been seeking all along was within, and since my body stored the journeys it had made, it was waiting to be one of my greatest teachers.

Yoga has been central to my ongoing work and has given rise to *The Guru is You: A Guide to Yoga for Self-Discovery and Purposeful Living*, a book that fuses yogic philosophy, self-study, practice methods, and lived experiences as a map for off-the-mat wellness for others to use. This book, *Body as Teacher: Yoga's Physical Practices for All*, has been a labor of love for my body and all people seeking an on-the-mat yoga exploration that weaves together poses and pose variations for all bodies (standing, seated, reclining, and chair-based practices), along with breathing techniques, subtle energy practices, meditation, and movements from multiple lineages.

Together, these books offer a combination of whole person wellness, creativity, inspiration, awareness, and inner evolution called Fusion Yoga Method. The term teacher is used throughout, as teaching that empowers others has profound impacts, while instruction of self-discovery is often limited.

The greatest teacher you will ever meet is yourself.

*C*hapter *1*
Foundation

Your body is your greatest physical teacher.

This book is streamlined so that your body
has what it needs to teach you something new every day.
You don't need to know yoga, speak Sanskrit or be flexible to begin.

Whether you are a beginner or seasoned practitioner, yoga teacher, or health professional,
you are invited to take from this book what serves you in this moment.

For those of you seeking a yoga practice that welcomes you,
no matter how your body and mind show up each day,
I sincerely hope this book supports that freedom.

Terms and principles used in this book evolved over thousands of years.
For deeper exploration, you might enjoy this book's companion, *The Guru is You: Yoga for Self-Discovery
and Purposeful Living.*

Practice, Learn, Teach

"The hard path to the easy life" – Countless yoga teachers.

Creating a yoga practice that promotes body, mind, and spirit wellness in one hour is quite an endeavor. Even if you are seasoned across many disciplines, it can be challenging to create sequences that are physically and energetically beneficial and draw on ancient philosophy in universal ways to promote mental health . . . while also leaving space for self-discovery and one's inner wisdom.

How closely an hour-long sequence meets these aims is typically related to the depth of a teacher's personal practice, study, and the physical lessons learned through personal or observed experience. The same is true for at-home practitioners developing daily practices. However, if all yogis could create well-rounded sequences more easily, more beneficial yoga would be accessible every day and everywhere.

Among the many yoga classes I've attended as a student, most have offered some space for mental and emotional wellness, less have offered space for one's connection to inner wisdom, and many less have led sequences that promote well-rounded physical wellness. Teaching yoga is hard in that it aims for holistic wellness in individual ways, often in a dynamic group environment. Compounding this challenge, many yoga teachers may not understand the importance of functional musculoskeletal sequences.

Ashtanga Foundation Poses in this book begin with a modified Ashtanga Primary Series that can be foundational for learning poses and variations. The series also has flaws in terms of physical wellness, but it can be used to analyze joint actions and opposing muscle actions for better understanding of musculoskeletal system basics.

Viewing poses through the lens of musculoskeletal actions can spotlight where and when to tighten and/or lengthen muscles and utilize joint actions in pose sequencing, and how to avoid unintentional neglect of important muscle groups and the loading of joints unevenly over time. Sequencing that somewhat balances major joint actions and opposing muscle groups can greatly contribute to musculoskeletal wellness.

In this book, you will find charts of joint actions and opposing muscle actions at the end of each Ashtanga Primary Series section, and practice teaching exercises at the end of most pose category sections that interlace new poses, breathing techniques, mudras, drishtis, bandhas and guided meditations with themes for wellness that can positively impact your daily life.

These practice exercises also invite you to fuse these yogic techniques into short classes to teach others. Though teaching yoga is not necessary, it can hold true that "If you really want to learn, then teach." Sharing yoga can expand awareness in new ways that are not obvious in individual practice. All teaching is recommended to be "off the mat" so that the teacher can be a student of everyone present, including themselves. Off the mat simply means not primarily reading off notes and demonstrating poses, as both of those actions can turn your attention away from other's experience and limit everyone's growth.

Wellness for All

The notion that one must be well to practice wellness limits everyone.

According to the CDC in 2024, 18% of adults in the United States report difficulty with mobility, and according to the WHO in 2023, 16% of people globally report significant mobility challenges. For many of these people, the physical practice of yoga can feel inaccessible. And in many cases, this stems from the reality that many yoga teachers receive minimal training in modifications and so tell students with mobility challenges, "ask your doctor which poses are right for you and only do what feels good."

Meanwhile, many doctors advise patients to do yoga for their condition unaware of differing physical yoga practices or that many yoga teachers lack basic understanding of functional anatomy. So often people that need yoga show up to their first class and receive negative reinforcement of their fears and pain.

The result is often "I tried it and yoga's not for me."

Every person who wishes to have a life-long physical yoga practice will need to one day adjust how they practice for continued benefit. My own pain and challenged mobility have led me down a path of discovery that included anatomy training, chiropractors, massage therapists, shamans, acupuncturists, surgeons and doctors, and physical and mental health therapists. What I've learned and experienced has informed this book's pose variations, which are meant to serve all bodies in individual ways – as it has been my personal experience that one-size-fits-all modifications do not result in optimum benefits. For example, for some poses, I need no variations; for other poses, a gentle variation works best; for still others, a reclining or chair variation is helpful.

Gentle Variations

Often for beginner yogis with mobility conditions, gentle variations of poses can offer a renewed sense of well-being. Gentle doesn't mean poses are not challenging; the name typically implies less tension on joints, tendons, and ligaments. Using gentle variations of poses together, such as in Sun Salutations, can remove any need to transition from the floor to standing, or vice versa. So, gentle variations of poses can allow those with joint conditions, osteoporosis, pregnancy, etc. to be included in group classes. Moreover, gentle variations can empower practitioners to continue mobility practices at home for medical and/or personal reasons.

Chair Variations

Chair variations of poses can also provide great benefits while supporting a safe, embodied sense of alignment for most anyone. However, people with certain back conditions and other spinal or hip flexion limitations may require additional props, such as a 2nd chair in front of them or other props for stability in more structurally aligned pose variations. This book consciously offers chair variations that are suitable for those unable to stand unaided to be inclusive of those without use of lower limbs. Again, a mixed mobility group class can include those who benefit from some or all poses while seated in a chair.

P*rop* V*ariations*

The use of props is highly recommended for most poses and can generally be used in any variation of the pose. This philosophy is based upon Iyengar principles mentioned earlier as props can help to reduce risks, maximize benefits, and increase longevity of practice. For example, using a block in revolved poses helps practitioners to not over-revolve too low in the spine. The lumbar spine is not designed to twist; it is designed to keep you upright. Another example is sitting in Easy Pose with a folded blanket under the tailbone to allow a stable posture for those with pelvic tilt, hip, or back conditions. Allowing a stable posture can strengthen the back, while rounding of the spine can result in further weakness. Prior to any group class or personal practice, plan and prepare for props so they can be fluidly integrated as needed.

R*eclining* V*ariations*

Reclining variations of poses in this book were designed to provide options for those unable to sit or stand, those desiring to use poses as stretches while in bed or on a massage table (which I did during surgical recovery periods), or as a progressive step to learn energetics of poses without distractions. Some physical techniques required in very challenging poses can be easily embodied from a reclining position. So in a group class, offering everyone the reclining variation first can provide both foundational learning for advancement and knowledge of a safe and beneficial place to return to if needed.

A*rm* V*ariations*

Sometimes the only variations that may be needed or desired are arm variations. Certain sequences, including Ashtanga's Sun Salutations, result in more shoulder flexion than the shoulder joints other actions. And some people with large chests and/or upper body muscles have discomfort in certain arm positions, thus detracting from the other benefits of the pose they are performing. Including arm variations in a group class or in your own practice can promote both mind-body connection and shoulder health.

A*dvanced* V*ariations*

Though nearly 20% of the population has mobility challenges, the other 80% have not yet been faced or are not currently faced with these challenges. It is also essential for practices to be inclusive of these people. This book includes the "full" version of each pose, which often requires an advanced yoga practice, as well as sometimes offering a step beyond. Teaching all variations of poses in this book is possible in one group setting because cueing for poses and variations is similar once the body understands each variation's felt experience.

Yoga best serves all bodies when it is applied with awareness and intention of individualized well-being. If you have any health conditions, please check with your doctor before beginning any physical practice meant to improve your overall wellness. The following general list of typical health conditions and corresponding recommendations for yoga practice can be a starting point to explore variations of poses for specific needs.

Health Conditions

This general list does not include all conditions or all recommendations for conditions mentioned. Each physical practice technique in this book also includes cautions that may provide further insight.

High Blood Pressure
* Limit breathing that increases internal heat (ex. Breath of Fire, Right Nostril).
* Limit excessive heat (ex. room temp, breath to movement vinyasa, etc.).
* Focus on grounding poses and breathing techniques that cool (ex. Seated Twist, Sitali).
* Lessen inversion height and angles of heart to head (ex. Legs Up the Wall vs Handstand)

Knee Conditions
* Focus on full leg strengthening poses that do not weight the knee joints (ex. Locust).
* Limit weighted knee flexion and rotation (ex. adjust stance, stay high in chair and squat).
* Offer options for both feet on the ground (ex. instead of W3, offer Half Pyramid).
* If using Vinyasa or Sun Salutations, start from the back of the mat rather than front.

Back Conditions
* Focus on back strength, reduce back stretching (ex. more Reverse Plank, less Forward Bends).
* Cue energetics of lengthening the spine with core stabilization (rather than rounding).
* Use props that support the spine (ex. wall or dowel while standing, bolsters for sitting).
* Limit revolved poses (twists) and use small step progression after generous warm up.
* If using reclined spinal twists, maintain both feet on the ground.
* If using Vinyasa or Sun Salutations, start from the back of the mat rather than front.

Shoulder and Wrist Conditions
* Offer optional arm positions (ex. Tall Mountain with cactus arms instead of arms up).
* Use blocks under hands for lift, support, and alignment (ex. Downward Dog).
* Offer stretches that gently rotate all arm joints at the same time (ex. Spreading Feathers).
* Avoid inversions that weight shoulders and wrists (ex. Legs Up the Wall instead of Handstand).
* If using Vinyasa or Sun Salutations, start from the back of the mat rather than front.

Chronic Fatigue and Fibromyalgia
* Vinyasa may be intolerable, movement must be gradual, or conditions may worsen.
* Begin with floor supported stretching and awareness of breath before active poses.

Sacroiliitis of SI Instability
* Focus on strengthening glutes, core, and lateral leg muscles rather than stretches (ex. more Squats, Bridges and Side Planks; stabilize Forward Bends or "hip openers").
* Stabilize (limit movement in pelvis) in one-legged (forward, back, or up) poses.
* If using Vinyasa or Sun Salutations, start from the back of the mat rather than front.

Amputees or Congenital Limb Conditions

- Counter repetitive daily life movements by strengthening opposing muscle groups.
- Rather than cueing limbs, cue energetics (ex. draw strength inward and upward).

Obesity

- Use props to shorten distances to allow full experience of body connection.
- More energetic poses and less reclining poses (Ayurvedic principle for excess Kapha).
- If using Vinyasa or Sun Salutations, start from the back of the mat rather than front.

Memory Loss or Brain Conditions

- Begin slowly and with repetition, be prepared to offer gentle assists to guide.
- Focus on supported balancing poses and engage bandhas (including feet and hands).
- Utilize Kundalini Yoga kriyas for specific conditions and/or focus on meditation.

Osteoporosis & Older Adults

- Focus on weight bearing and balancing poses to stimulate bone strength.
- Emphasis slowing down and lengthening of the spine to counter collapsing into poses.
- Include gentle backbends, mild side bends, and restorative poses.
- Use props to support decreased cartilage, bone density, balance, and circulation.
- Modify Vinyasa or Salutations with a chair or wall and limit transitions to the floor.
- AVOID these poses that decrease spine stability in those with lower bone density:
    - ☒ Forward folds (ex. Forward Bend and rolling up to stand)
    - ☒ Moderate to deep twists (ex. Revolved Triangle)
    - ☒ Lumbar flexion (ex. Cat)
    - ☒ Deep backbends (ex. Wheel) and big inversions (ex. Head Stand)
    - ☒ Big stretches (ex. Pigeon)
    - ☒ Big neck extensions or flexions (ex. Fish or Shoulder Stand)

Prenatal

- After the first trimester pre-natal, and up to 8 weeks post-partum,
  AVOID these poses counter to natural body temp, internal space, and weighted spine stability.
    - ☒ Forward folds (ex. Forward Bend and Seated Forward Folds)
    - ☒ Spinal flexions (ex. Cow) or big spinal extensions (ex. Wheel)
    - ☒ Revolved poses (ex. Revolved Lunge)
    - ☒ Deep hip stretches (ex. Pigeon)
    - ☒ Deep inversions (ex. Handstand, Plow, and Shoulder Stand)
    - ☒ Belly down poses (ex. Cobra) or lying flat on back (ex. Savasana)
    - ☒ Hot yoga and breathing that elevates blood pressure (ex. Breath of Fire)

PTSD

- Hands on assists, darkness and facing away from the exit may be intolerable.
- Offer alternative poses to Child's Pose, Savasana and others that resemble helplessness.

Somatic Alignment

Be present for the teacher (your body's experience).

Your body includes your mind, yet your thoughts can be in discord with physical characteristics, actions, or sensations. Your body is your best friend, yet at times you might barely recognize it. Everything that happens in your life is recorded by your body, yet it can unlearn and gather new information each day of existence.

This paradoxical relationship is often what brings people to yoga.

Yogic practices can improve physical posture and strength, as well as nervous system resilience, while also offering pain relief and a sense of whole person connection. Yoga's relationships to the nervous system is explored more in depth in this book's companion, *The Guru is You: Yoga for Self-Discovery and Purposeful Living*. Mind and body benefits can be optimized by adapting or modifying poses for everyone's unique presentation through Iyengar methodology combined with somatic awareness for internal receptivity and improved neuroplasticity. In essence, one's physical position can significantly impact physical, mental, and emotional wellness.

Iyengar Focus

B.K.S. Iyengar was a student of Tirumalai Krishnamacharya at a Hatha yoga school in 1934 in Mysore, India. As a child, B.K.S. Iyengar faced poverty, malnourishment, influenza, malaria, tuberculosis, and typhoid fever. And although Krishnamacharya invited Iyengar to his Hatha School, Iyengar was expected to do poorly in asana (poses) due to his condition and would mostly help with chores around the school. Iyengar notes in his book, *Light on Yoga*, that he received little formal training; but it was enough time to change his life.

Iyengar went on to develop his own style of yoga focused on reducing risks and maximizing benefits in the practice of poses using props, functional sequencing, and precise cueing. An Iyengar teacher would not say to a student having trouble in any pose to "do what works for your body today" without also offering options to help someone investigate what that means for them.

Somatic yoga practice was developed outside of yoga and has its roots in the Alexander Technique principle of "stop doing what interferes with natural coordination," the Feldenkrais Method principle of "movement is a dialogue with the nervous system," and Thomas Hanna's coining of the term Somatic practices meaning *Somatic Experience* that which helps our brains to let go of those pre-conditioned thoughts not supportive of our wellness. So, somatic practice and Iyengar's methodology together focus on mindfulness about where body parts are and what sensations (other than sight) are experienced for positive connections between mind and body (nervous and musculoskeletal systems).

The Roots of Yoga Practice

Yoga's origins can be traced back to ancient Vedic philosophy of mind-body-spirit connection. Yoga then went through 2,000 years of theory and practice expansion before Sage Patanjali complied the *Yoga Sutras* on palm leaves to demystify Raja Yoga, the yoga of meditation. These palm leaves outline parts or limbs of practice that in combination can promote one's most meaningful experience of life. The 8 limbs of yoga are:

Yamas

Universal Ethics

Non-violence, truthfulness, non-stealing, moderation, non-hoarding

Samadhi

Transcendence

Liberation from mind fluctuations / bliss.

Niyamas

Inner disciplines

Cleanliness, contentment, self-discipline, self-study, celebration of spirit

Dhyana

Meditation

Keen awareness without focus. Being rather than doing.

Asana

Physical Postures

Body readiness to sit in meditation.

Dharana

Deep Concentration

Single-pointed focus.

Pranayama

Regulation of Life Force

Control of breath for self-regulation.

Pratyahara

Mastering the External

Consciously drawing awareness from the external to the internal.

Over time yoga became more associated with Asana (poses) than the other limbs. And now many classes offer practices primarily comprised of poses. This narrowing of yoga can be confusing, as limiting context often renders a system less useful overall. For example, a question that often arises for beginning practitioners is why is meditation so important in yoga?

Hatha yoga emerged from tantric practices and philosophies that worked with mind–body energetics from early yogic traditions, including Raja yoga with its roots in the Vedas. So, in yoga's lineage, Hatha and Raja yoga intersect in that both use practices to prepare one for meditation. And in the *Yoga Sutras*, Patanjali explains the greatest benefits of yoga include the mind being yoked back to personal clarity.

Neither Hatha nor Raja yoga are intended to be primarily practices of poses. Another misunderstanding can be that Hatha yoga means a slower sequence or one that does not include ancient philosophies. However, Hatha does include yoga's philosophical framework and Hatha classes can be any pace. For example, forms of asana that fall under Hatha include Vinyasa, Power, Anusara, Gentle, Kundalini, Yin, Bikram, Ashtanga, etc.

The *Yoga Sutras* (associated with Raja yoga) predates major Hatha yoga texts by more than a thousand years, offering the framework for meditation and yogic philosophies that Hatha's methods support. Hatha yoga includes methods that support the overall aims of Raja yoga, including:

> *P*oses *(Asana)*
>
> *B*reath regulation *(Pranayama)*
>
> *E*nergetic techniques *(Bandhas, Mudras)*
>
> *S*ubtle energy and focus practices *(Drishtis, Mantra, etc.)*
>
> *C*leansing methods *(Shatkarmas)*

The techniques in this book include all of these Hatha yoga's focus areas with the exception of cleansing methods. Ayurveda's more natural seasonal cleanse technique is explored in this book's companion; *The Guru is You: Yoga for Self-Discovery and Purposeful Living.*

Practice

Adapting the Ashtanga Vinyasa yoga practice sequence can be a foundation for learning asana through variations that engage similar energetics.

1. Experiment
    a) Review Sun Salutation A in the Ashtanga Primary Series Poses section.
    b) Practice variations of Sun Salutation A poses until you find the variations of each pose that offer you a renewed sense of physical strength and mental resilience at this moment.
    c) Review the Health Conditions list and choose one or more that you have interest in, then review the Sun Salutation A pose through that condition's lens and consider other pose variations that may help someone with that condition feel more resilient.

2. Move

    Take a class labeled as Gentle yoga. Before and after class, note sensations in your body.

    Before: My heart feels ___________, my head feels __________, my feet feel ___________.

    After: My heart feels ___________, my head feels __________, my feet feel ___________.

Subtle Energy

"The visible world is the invisible organization of energy" - Heinz Pagels.

This book also identifies Vayus (energy directions), Chakras (energy centers), and Doshas (primary energy influences) for most all physical practice techniques included. If you desire an exploration into Vayus, Doshas and Chakras, this book's companion, *The Guru is You: Yoga for Self-Discovery and Purposeful Living*, offers more depth in these areas.

Vayus   Vayus are derived from early Vedic texts that told stories and provided insight into how to direct internal forces for increased physical and mental alignment. In general, the term Vayu is Sanskrit for winds or flows of bodily energy. Vayus can help with creating more effective sequences towards practice aims and modifying poses while achieving similar benefits. The primary vayus are:

Prana	pulling energy *inward* (air/inspiration to head and heart).
Apana	releasing energy *downward* (grounding).
Samana	moving energy for *balancing* (stabilizing).
Udana	pushing energy *upward* (expression and growth).
Vyana	expanding energy *outward* (circulating and integrating).

Chakras   Chakras are traced back to the early Upanishads and show up in Ayurveda, the *Yoga Sutras*, Hinduism, and Buddhism. Chakra means wheel in Sanskrit and our subtle anatomy includes these psychological/physiological development energetic centers. Life influences or experiences can alter energy in our bodies, resulting in stored energy (creating an excess) or avoidant energy (creating a deficiency) in the chakra most impacted by life events or other stressors. When it comes to deficiency or excess chakra energy, one is not better than the other. What shows up is simply an indicator of what processing tools were most available to one at the time. This book focuses on Hatha's 7 main chakras for insight into energetic techniques that can help one feel more balanced and resilient. Most practice methods list the chakras most balanced by that method, which are:

Root	*Exist* (tailbone, security)
Sacral	*Feel* (pelvis, authenticity)
Solar Plexus	*Act* (navel, self-esteem)
Heart	*Love* (chest, compassion)
Throat	*Truth* (throat, expression)
3rd Eye	*Vision* (brow center, trust)
Crown	*Connection* (top of head, unity)

D*oshas* In yoga's sister science of Ayurveda, Doshas (patterns of energy in the body and mind, also called Prakriti). Ayurveda is traced back to the *Rig* and *Atharva* Vedas that outline 3 doshas with differences in thoughts, emotions, and physical states. According to Ayurveda, when one's natural state is disrupted by stressors, subtle energy blockages can occur.

In a nutshell, when external forces in one's life disturb one's internal harmony, one's energy changes . . . impacting mood, bodily systems, sleep, weight, and more. Using doshic considerations in yoga means consciously directing vayus as needed for increased harmony by using "pacifying" energetic techniques. Most practice methods in this book state which doshas it pacifies, and some may state all except doshas with excess. In Ayurveda, like draws like, so if one is experiencing a disruption to their harmony, often it is because they are experiencing too many like qualities of the energy already in their mind and body, so what is needed is other elemental balance. The 3 Doshas with their general pacifying techniques are:

Vata *Air & Ether qualities* (warm, slow pace, increase stability, establish grounding)

Pitta *Fire & Water qualities* (cool, less tension, moderate effort, increase relaxation)

Kapha *Earth & Water qualities* (warm, energize, challenge, circulate, release emotion)

Awareness of vayus, chakras and doshas can inform practice sequences and impact the benefits of your personal practice when you know which Dosha and Chakras you are seeking more balance in.

Chapter 2
Ashtanga Poses

"Practice is not about perfection.
It's about progress"
- Sharath Jois.

The Ashtanga Primary Series falls under Hatha yoga. Hatha emerged from Tantric practices that worked with mind–body energetics and shares roots with Raja yoga (philosophical origins in the Vedas). A preset sequence inspired by the Ashtanga Primary Series can be foundational for Hatha practice. This chapter offers the following fundamental aspects towards that endeavor:

Linking poses together
Varying paces of poses
Joint and muscle actions in poses
Variations of poses for optimum wellness
Subtle energy practices (breathing, drishti, bandhas, mantras)

The Physical Practice of Ashtanga Yoga

The first Hatha yoga school opened in 1920 in Mysore, India, where teacher Krishnamacharya designed a demanding sequence for student Patthabi Jois. Jois then added poses to his teacher's sequence and named it Ashtanga. The resulting set sequence has been practiced around the world ever since and can be led either by a teacher (who does not practice) or in the Mysore method (an open practice). The Ashtanga series can be practiced as a Primary Series, Intermediate, or Advance Series. This book focuses on the Ashtanga Primary Series, which includes the following distinct categories of poses in this order:

- ✓ Sun Salutations A
- ✓ Sun Salutations B
- ✓ Standing Series
- ✓ Seated and Finishing Series

In general, Ashtanga practice has 5 main principles:
- ✓ Ujjayi (breathing technique)
- ✓ Drishti (eye focus)
- ✓ Vinyasa (placing things in a special way while matching breath to movement)
- ✓ Bandhas (energetic locks)
- ✓ Daily practice (rest days are Saturday, full and new moon, and menstrual days)

Ashtanga practice birthed vinyasa (or "flow") type of yoga as it provides a foundation for linking breath to movement. Linking Ujjayi breath to poses and transitions can promote a more symbiotic relationship between the nervous and musculoskeletal systems for increased health and resilience. Drishti, or directing attention toward a point with a softness dispels distractions and judgements can increase positive energy flow. Bandhas, energy locks within our power, can increase stability, mentally, physically, and emotionally. Using Ujjayi, Drishti, Vinyasa, and Bandhas with poses render the Ashtanga sequence, and many other physical sequences, far more potent than body movements alone. You can learn more about breathing techniques, eye gazes, and energetic locks in this book's Subtle Energy chapter.

As far as daily practice, the *Yoga Sutras* 1.14. states that consistent practice over a long period strengthens samskaras (mental impressions) by improving positive thought processes and responses to stress that can remodel samsara (hamster wheel of pre-conditioned existence). Consistent practice does not mean only poses, breathing, energy locks, and eye gazes. For more about the other limbs of yoga and off-the-mat practices, check out this book's companion, *The Guru is You: Yoga for Self-Discovery and Purposeful Living*.

Unfortunately, teacher Patthabi Jois harmed students with violence, which is not in alignment with yoga at all. So, while I share the benefits of Ashtanga's physical practice and use it as a bedrock for developing sequences, the modified Ashtanga Primary Sequence shared in this book leaves out some Seated and Finishing poses that can risk functional wellness and have the potential of creating more harm than good.

ASHTANGA PRIMARY SERIES INSPIRED CLASS

Asana is a steady, stable and comfortable posture"
- Sutra 2. 46.

✓ Pose # shown reflects where it appears in this chapter.
✓ Some yogis combine Half Lift as a transition to Limbed Staff Pose.
✓ Traditionally, no music is played - cadence is breath.
✓ Teacher counts 1– Ekam; 2 Dve; 3 Treen; 4 Chatvarri; and 5 Pancha

Opening Chant (stand at Mountain at the top of the mat, see chant under Subtle Energy/Mantra)

Sun Salutation A – Repeat 5x (Ujjayi breath to movement except 5 breaths in Downward Dog)
1. Inhale/Exhale - Mountain - Samasthiti
2. Inhale - Tall Mountain - Ūrdhva Hastāsana
3. Exhale - Forward Fold - Uttānāsana
4. Inhale - Half Lift - Ardha Uttānāsana
5. Exhale - 4 Limbed Staff Pose - Chaturanga Dandāsana
6. Inhale - Up Dog - Ūrdhva Mukha Śvānāsana
7. Exhale Downward Dog - Adho Mukha Śvānāsana
4. Inhale - Half Lift - Ardha Uttānāsana
3. Exhale - Forward Fold - Uttānāsana
2. Inhale - Tall Mountain - Ūrdhva Hastāsana
1. Exhale - Mountain – Tādāsana

Sun Salutation B – Repeat 5x (Ujjayi breath to movement except 5 Ujjayi breaths in Downward Dog)
8. Inhale (from Mountain) - Chair - Utkatāsana
3. Exhale - Forward Fold - Uttānāsana
4. Inhale - Half Lift - Ardha Uttānāsana
5. Exhale - 4 Limbed Staff Pose - Chaturanga Dandāsana
6. Inhale - Up Dog - Ūrdhva Mukha Śvānāsana
7. Exhale - Down Dog - Adho Mukha Śvānāsana
9. Inhale - Warrior 1 (right) - Vīrabhadrāsana I
5. Exhale - 4 Limbed Staff Pose - Chaturanga Dandāsana
6. Inhale - Up Dog - Ūrdhva Mukha Śvānāsana
7. Exhale - Down Dog - Adho Mukha Śvānāsana
9. Inhale - Warrior 1 (left)
5. Exhale - 4 Limbed Staff Pose - Chaturanga Dandāsana
6. Inhale - Up Dog - Ūrdhva Mukha Śvānāsana
7. Exhale - Down Dog - Adho Mukha Śvānāsana
4. Inhale - Half Lift - Ardha Uttānāsana
3. Exhale - Forward Fold - Uttānāsana
8. Inhale - Chair - Utkatāsana
1. Exhale - Mountain – Tādāsana

Standing Series – 1x each (5 Ujjayi breaths each pose, each side)
10. Big Toe – Padangushtasana
11. Hand under foot pose - Pada Hastasana
12. 5-Pointed Star Variation – Utthita Tadasana (a.k.a Step Back)
13. Extended Triangle - Utthita Trikonasana
14. Revolved Triangle - Parivritta Trikonasana
1. Mountain (a.k.a Step to Top of Mat)
12. 5-Pointed Star Variation – Utthita Tadasana (a.k.a Step Back)
15. Extended Side Angle - Utthita Parshvakonasana

16. Revolved Side Angle - Parivritta Parshvakonasana
1. Mountain (a.k.a Step to Top of Mat)
12. 5-Pointed Star Variation – Utthita Tadasana (a.k.a Step Back)
17. Wide Leg Forward Fold - Prasarita Padottanasana A
    Wide Leg Forward Fold - Prasarita Padottanasana B
    Wide Leg Forward Fold - Prasarita Padottanasana C
    Wide Leg Forward Fold - Prasarita Padottanasana D
1. Mountain (a.k.a Step to Top of Mat)
18. Pyramid/Reverse Namaste – Parshvottanasana (pivot between sides, then step back to top)
19. Leg Extended - Utthita Hasta Padangushtasana A
    Leg Extended - Utthita Hasta Padangushtasana B
    Leg Extended - Utthita Hasta Padangushtasana D
20. Half Bound Lotus - Ardha Baddha Padmottanasana
8. Chair – Utkatanasana
3. Exhale - Forward Fold - Uttānāsana
4. Inhale - Half Lift - Ardha Uttānāsana
5. Exhale - 4 Limbed Staff Pose - Chaturanga Dandāsana
6. Inhale - Up Dog - Urdhva Mukha Śvānāsana
7. Exhale - Down Dog - Adho Mukha Śvānāsana
9. Warrior 1 - Virabhadrasana I (pivot between sides, then step back to top after both sides complete)
21. Warrior 2 - Virabhadrasana II (pivot between sides, then step back to top after both sides complete)
22. Crow Pose

Seated Series – 1x each (Both sides when applicable, 5 Breaths each)
23. Transition to Staff
24. Seated Straight Legged/Staff – Dandasana
25. Seated Forward Fold – Paschimattanasana A
    Seated Forward Fold – Paschimattanasana B
26. Reverse Plank - Purvatanasana
23. Transitions to/from Staff
27. Seated Half bound (down) Lotus - Janu Shirshasana A
23. Transition from Janu A on right to Janu A on left, then transition from Janu A to Staff
28. Sage Twist – Marichyasana C
23. Transition from Mari C on right to Mari C on left, then transition from Mari C to Staff
29. Boat Pose
23. Transition from Boat to Staff
30. Bound Angle - Baddha Konasana

Finishing Series (5-10 Breaths each, except 5-10 min in Savasana)
31. Bridge - Setu Bandhasana Sarvangasana
32. Wheel - Urdhva Dhanurasana
33. Shoulder Stand – Sarvangasana
34. Plow – Halasana
35. Fish - Uttana Padasana
36. Dolphin or Forearm Stand
37. Child's Pose – Balasana
38. Corpse pose – Savasana

Closing Chant (standing at Mountain at the top of the mat, see chant under Subtle Energy/Mantra)

Sun Salutation A

"How glorious a greeting the sun gives the mountains!" — John Muir.

In the Ashtanga Primary Series, practice begins with Sun Salutation A (often called Sun A) is 5 repetitions using Ujjayi in breath to movement, except for 5 breath count holds in Downward Dog. Sun A can decrease tension, improve circulation, stimulate the nervous system, increase body heat and metabolism, lubricate joints, strengthen muscles, and soothe fascia. Important notes for this Ashtanga Primary Series Sun Salutation A are:

- ✓ When using Sun A in Ashtanga, follow the "Ashtanga Primary Series Inspired Class" outline.
- ∗ When sequencing these poses in <u>other</u> than the Ashtanga preset sequence, refer to "Sequence" ideas, and for poses listed that are two-sided poses, repeat on left side.
- ✓ If a practitioner is without use of one or more limbs, modify variations to engage available joints.
- ✓ In Chair Plank, Reclining Plank and Downward Dog, both legs can lift upward. However, those with lower back conditions (injury, pregnancy, osteoporosis, SI dysfunction, etc.) can decrease risk of lower back issues by lifting one leg at a time and alternating leg in front/lifted as the pose is repeated.
- ✓ Cautions presented cannot cover all variables and are not a substitute for medical advice.
- ✓ The image on the next page shows how Sun A can be used in a mixed mobility group class.

Advanced Sun A (for all-levels class, offer Plank instead of mid-plank and Cobra instead of Upward Dog)
Gentle/Standing Sun A Variation (alternate front leg in standing Downward Dog)
Chair Sun A Variation (alternate lifted leg in chair Plank)
Prop Sun A Variation
Reclining Sun A Variation (alternate lifted leg in reclining Plank and reclining Downward Dog)

1. **Mountain – Tadasana** (Tada = mountain)

    Chakras/Doshas/Vayus.   Root/All/Balancing, expanding, downward, upward.

    Cautions.   None

    Benefits.   Strengthens whole body and can improve posture and focus.

    Cues.   Align ears, shoulders, hips, and ankles.

    Arms at sides, palms face out, collarbones broaden, shoulders relax.

    Spread toes, press foot corners downward, lift arches.

    Tailbone is neutral, core draws inward/upward, spine lengthens.

    Sequence*. Tall Mountain, Tree, Eagle, Warrior III, or Qigong Knock.

    Variations.   Arms in prayer hands.

    In chair, engage sit bones and feet downward.

    Block between thighs, squeeze inward and backward.

    Recline with feet flexed, back body presses downward and outward.

2. **Tall Mountain – Urdhva Hastasana** (Urdhva = raised, Hasta = hand)

    Chakras/Doshas/Vayus.   Root, Heart/All/Balancing, expanding, upward.

    Cautions.   Shoulder conditions.

    Benefits.   Strengthens the whole body. Can increase energy and alertness.

    Cues.   (From Mountain) Inhale and reverse swan dive arms upward.

    Palms face, shoulder blades travel down spine.

    Feet press down; navel draws inward towards spine.

    Sequence*. Forward Bend, Radiance Charger, Palm Tree, Standing Splits.

    Variations.   Arms in Cactus shape.

    Chair Mountain, upper half lifts upward.

    Block between thighs and hands (press both inward).

    Recline in Mountain, arms overhead, shoulders and thumbs on floor.

3. **Forward Bend/Fold – Uttanasana** (Ut = intense, Tan= to stretch or extend)

Chakras/Doshas/Vayus. Crown/Vata and Pitta/Downward, upward.

Cautions.	Lower back/SI joints. Avoid anterior disc compression by NOT "rolling up."
Benefits.	Stretches back side of body, can reduce anxiety and stimulate digestion.
Cues.	(From Tall Mountain) Exhale to swan dive arms while hinging at waist.
	Hands come to ground; knees are slightly bent.
	Naval draws towards spine, and chest towards thighs.
	Head relaxes downward, gaze towards knees.
Sequence*.	Half Lift, Chair Pose, Closed-leg Squat, Kundalini Frog.
Variations.	Standing Seal or Wide Legged Forward Bend.
	In chair, sit forward on chair edge to perform.
	Hands on block or other object for support.
	Recline with knees bent inward, head and shoulders on ground

4. **Half lift – Ardha Uttanasana** (Ardha = half, Ut = intense, Tan = stretch)

Chakras/Doshas/Vayus. Root, Solar/All/Downward, balancing.

Cautions.	Lower back and pre-natal.
Benefits.	Strengthens core and stretches backs of legs.
	Can improve posture and digestion.
Cues.	(From Forward Bend) Inhale to raise torso upward.
	Hands remain on floor or slide up to chins, spine is straight.
	Broaden collarbones, narrow space between shoulder blades.
	Press hamstrings backward, crown forward, gaze forward of mat.
Sequence*.	Plank, Balancing Half Moon, Runner's Lunge, Forward Bend.
Variations.	Hands higher on legs, widen stance, or slightly bend knees with airplane arms.
	In chair, bring hands to thighs, bend elbows to engage back.
	Hands on two blocks or wall for support
	Recline with legs straight up, hands behind thighs.

5. **Plank – Dandasana / Kumbhakasana** (Dandasana = staff, Kumbhak = breath retention)

Chakras/Doshas/Vayus. Root, Solar/All/Downward, balancing, expanding.

Cautions. Wrist and shoulder conditions.

Benefits. Strengthen core, arms and back.

Can increase stamina and energy.

Cues. (From Half Lift) Exhale feet back to straight legs.

Shoulders are over wrists, elbows hug inward.

Heels press back, hamstrings and glutes lift.

Core and thighs are strong and steady.

Knuckles press downward, shoulder blades flatten outward.

Back of neck is long, gaze is down and forward.

Sequence*. Forearm Plank, Upward Dog, Cobra, Side Plank, Downward Dog.

Variations. Standing Chair pose, arms forward and wrists flexed.

Straight arms (not overextended) and/or one leg lifted.

Knees Down Plank, Forearm Plank, or Hovering Table (knees lift).

In chair, extend one leg and both arms outward, feet flex, switch lifted leg on repetitions.

In chair option of Reverse Plank.

Blocks for wrist support or perform at leaning into a wall.

Recline with arms upward; raise calves perpendicular to floor, alternate lifted leg on repetitions.

Back of the Mat Leverage

The general list of modifications in the previous chapter provided repeated this phrase for many health conditions, "if using Vinyasa or Sun Salutations, start from the back of the mat rather than front." Starting from the back of the mat is primarily to reduce weight and cumulative wear on your shoulder joints.

When starting from the front of the mat, your shoulder joints become a fixed anchor as the body moves into to plank (or Table) – meaning your shoulder joints bear and absorb most of your body weight. However, when the sequence starts from the back of the mat and you walk your hands forward to plank (or Table), the load shifts and your whole body participates to distribute effort more evenly.

Practicing Sun Salutations both ways (front to back and back to front) reveals that breath patterns and pose cues remain the same, making this option easy to integrate in any group practice without disrupting flow. Over time, hacks like this can have positive impacts on joint health and longevity of practice.

6. **Upward Facing Dog - Urdhva Mukha Svanasana** (Urdhva=upward, Mukha=face, Svana=dog)

   Chakras/Doshas/Vayus. Root, Sacral, Solar, Heart/All except Pitta Imbalance/All.

   Cautions.   Back conditions, osteoporosis and pre-natal.

   Benefits.   Strengthens core, buttocks, and thighs. Can decrease sciatica and stress.

   Cues.   (From Plank) Exhale to lower halfway, shift forward to tops of feet on mat.
   Torso and thighs engaged and lifted (not touching floor).
   Chest expands, collarbones broaden, shoulders press back and down.
   Neck lengthens, gaze is forward and up.

   Sequence*. Downward Dog, Child's Pose, Table.

   Variations.   Standing cactus arms, tilt chin upward.
   Cobra, Locust, or Cow.
   In chair, cactus arms, and tilt chin upward
   Bolster under low pelvis or blocks under hands.
   Reclining Cobra.

7. **Downward Facing Dog - Adho Mukha Svanasana** (Adho=downward; Mukha=face; Svana=dog)

   Chakras/Doshas/Vayus. All except Throat/All/Downward, balancing.

   Cautions.   Overuse can lead to instability. Do not hyperextend elbows.

   Benefits.   Stretches back of body. Can help with fatigue and stress.

   Cues.   (From Upward Dog) Exhale to tuck toes, lift tailbone up.
   Widen fingers (index forward), press fingers pads down.
   Micro bend knees, shoulder blades, and ribs broaden.

   Sequence*. Half Lift, Table, 3-Legged Dog; Forward Bend.

   Variations.   Stand, extend one leg, toes flex, lean into "V; or Half Pyramid.
   Puppy pose.
   In chair, legs straight, ankles and wrists flex, arms, and legs form "V."
   Blocks under hands.
   Recline, extend leg, toes flex, raise arms, wrists flex. raise arms, change leg on repetitions.

Practice

1. Breathe

Review Durga and Ujjayi breathing techniques in Pranayama. Practice each for 3 minutes.
Ask someone to let you practice guiding these breaths and you will both integrate the practices even more.

2. Teach

Review the Sun Salutation A poses. Practice each Sun A version a few times, leading with the breath cue provided. Then lead someone else through three versions of Sun Salutation A (lead a total of 3 Sun Salutations, each one of them will be different). Teach with minimal demonstration and without notes and stop at any pose that is not working and find a variation that provides maximum benefit.

After class, ask for the following feedback:

What did they see during class?

What did they hear during class?

What did they feel during class?

What was their overall experience of class?

What did they like best about your teaching?

What is one thing they could tell you to help you grow?

3. Move

Review and practice Hasta, Pada, and Uddiyana bandhas. Then take a class labeled Sun Salutations and use bandhas in your practice. Before and after class, note sensations in your body.

Before: My heart feels ___________, my head feels _________, my feet feel ___________.

After: My heart feels ___________, my head feels _________, my feet feel __________.

Sun Salutation B

"He who conquers himself is the mightiest warrior." – Confucius.

In the Ashtanga Primary Series, Sun Salutation B (often called Sun B) follows Sun A in another 5 repetitions using Ujjayi breathing in breath to movement, except for 5 breath counts in Downward Dog. Sun B provides additional stretching and strengthening and supports circulation, body heat/metabolism, and joint lubrication. Important notes for this Ashtanga Primary Series Sun Salutation B are:

- ✓ When using Sun B in Ashtanga, follow the "Ashtanga Inspired Class" outline.
- * When sequencing these poses in <u>other</u> than the Ashtanga sequence, refer to "Sequence" ideas; and for poses listed that are two-sided poses, repeat on left side.
- ✓ Cautions presented cannot cover all variables and are not a substitute for medical advice.
- ✓ If a practitioner is without use of one or more limbs, modify variations to engage available joints.
- ✓ In Chair Plank, and Reclining Plank/Downward Dog/Chair, both legs can lift upward. However, those with lower back conditions (including injury, pregnancy, osteoporosis, SI dysfunction, etc.) can decrease risk of lower back issues by lifting one leg at a time. If lifting one leg at a time, alternate which leg is in front or lifted as the pose is repeated throughout the sequence.
- ✓ In Chair, Reclining, and Standing versions of Sun Salutation B, the additional transitional pose of 5-Pointed Star is added prior to Warrior I for transition and alignment purposes.
- ✓ The image on the next page shows how Sun B can be used in a mixed mobility group class.

Advanced Sun B (for all levels class, offer Plank instead of Mid-Plank and Cobra instead of Upward Dog)

Gentle Sun B Variation (for smoother transitions, use 5-Star instead of Down Dogs before Warrior 1s, alternate leg in Down Dog)

Chair Sun B Variation (for smoother transitions, use 5-Star instead of Downward Dogs before Warrior 1s)

Prop Sun B Variation (for smoother transitions, use block in hands in Chair, under hands in Upward Dog, and in hands in Warrior 1s)

Reclining Sun B Variation (for smoother transitions, use 5-Star instead of Down Dogs before Warrior 1s, and change leg in Down Dog and Chair)

8. **Chair – Utkatasana** (Utkata = powerful or fierce)
   Chakras/Doshas/Vayus. Root, Solar Plexus/All except Pitta/Downward, balancing, upward.
   Cautions.   None.
   Benefits.   Strengthens legs, glutes, and core, and can increase stamina.
   Cues.   Inhale to bend knees and raise arms to "sit."
                      Tailbone draws downward, back stays long and tall.
                      Press into heels, engage back body, gaze forward or between hands.
   Sequence.   Plank, Mountain, Palm Tree, Qigong Heaven and Earth.
   Variations.   Prayer hands or hover arms perpendicular to floor; lessen bend in knees.
                      Sit in chair. press feet down, learn torso forward, raise arms upward.
                      Back against wall for support or squeeze block between thighs.
                      Recline with one or both arms upward, one knee bent (foot up/flexed),
                      other leg straight, alternate sides or lift both knees at same time.

9. **Warrior 1 - Virabhadrasana I** (Virabhadra = mythical Vedic deity)
   Chakras/Doshas/Vayus. Root, Sacral, Solar Plexus/All/All.
   Cautions.   Unnaturally squaring reduces stability (widen stance for natural angle).
   Benefits.   Can strengthen limbs and core and improve stamina and flexibility.
   Cues.   From Downward Dog, inhale right foot inside of right hand; OR,
                      Front knee is bent and above ankle, back foot angles to 45 degrees.
                      Adjust stance width for stability, equalize weight in feet.
                      Raise hands upward, ribs broaden, shoulders are low.
                      To continue sequence, exhale hands down, step back to plank.
   Sequence.   Down Dog, Runner's Lunge, Plank, Humble Warrior.
   Variations.   Shorter/wider stance, cactus arms.
                      Low Lunge with hip angled outward.
                      From Chair Star, slide right leg to right/left leg to left, straighten left knee.
                      Dowel between hands to further alignment.
                      Stack body on one side, recline in Half Bow pose.

Sun A and B Joint and Muscle Actions

Pose	Spine	Shoulders	Hips	Knees	Upper Front — Abdominals & fronts of arms, chest, shoulders — Contracts	Stretches	Upper Back — Mid/upper back & backs of arms, shoulders — Contracts	Stretches	Lower Front — Fronts of pelvis & legs, quads,hip flexors — Contracts	Stretches	Lower Back — Backs of legs, glutes, hamstrings — Contracts	Stretches	Side Body — Limbs out from sides (abduction), or into midline (adduction) — Adduction	Abduction
Ujjayi Breath	Neutral	Rotation	Neutral	Neutral	No	No	No	No	No	No	No	No	No	No
Mountain	Neutral	Rotation	Neutral	Neutral	No	No	No	No	No	No	No	No	No	No
Tall Mountain	Extension	Flexion	Neutral	Neutral	No	Yes	No	Yes	No	No	No	No	No	No
Forward Bend	Flexion	Flexion	Flexion	Neutral	Yes	No	No	Yes	Yes	No	No	Yes	No	No
Halfway Lift	Extension	Flexion	Flexion	Neutral	Yes	No	Yes	No	Yes	No	No	No	No	No
Plank	Neutral	Flexion	Neutral	Neutral	Yes	No	Yes	No	Yes	No	Yes	No	No	No
Mid-Plank	Neutral	Extension	Neutral	Neutral	Yes	No	Yes	No	Yes	No	Yes	No	No	No
Upward Dog	Extension	Extension	Extension	Neutral	No	Yes	Yes	No	No	Yes	Yes	No	No	No
Cobra	Extension	Extension	Neutral	Neutral	No	Yes	Yes	No	No	No	No	No	No	No
Down Dog	Neutral	Flex/Rot	Flexion	Neutral	Yes	No	No	Yes	Yes	No	No	Yes	No	No
Chair	Flexion	Flex/Rot	Flexion	Flexion	No	Yes	No	Yes	Yes	No	Yes	No	No	No
Warrior I	Extension	Flex/Rot	Flex/Ext/Abd/Rot	Flex/Rot	No	Yes	No	Yes	Yes	Yes	Yes	Yes	No	Yes
# Flexion	2	7	5	1										
# Extension	5	3	2	0										
# Rotation	0	4	1	1										
# Abduction		0	1											
# Adduction		0	0											
TOTAL # YES					5	5	5	5	7	2	5	3	0	1

Primary actions may be multiple (i.e., when legs or arms in differing directions from such as Warrior I).

Flexion	Decreasing angle.
Extension	Increasing angle.
Rotation	On axis inward or outward.
Abduction	Moving legs or arms out to sides from body.
Adduction	Moving legs or arms inward toward midline.
Contracts	Tensing or shortening under load
Stretches	Lengthening under load

Practice

1. Breathe

Review Sama Vritti and Segmented breathing techniques in Pranayama. Practice each breath for 3 minutes. Ask someone to let you practice guiding these breaths. Try teaching without notes to integrate more.

2. Teach

Review the two new poses in Sun Salutation B. Practice each version of the entire Sun Salutation B a few times, leading with the breath cue provided. Then lead someone else through 3 versions of Sun Salutation A and B (leading a total of 5 Sun Salutations A and B). Teach with minimal demonstration and without notes and stop at any pose that is not working and find a variation that provides maximum benefit.

After class, ask for the following feedback:

> What did they see during class?
> What did they hear during class?
> What did they feel during class?
> What was their overall experience of class?
> What did they like best about your teaching?
> What is one thing they could tell you to help you grow?

3. Joint Actions
   a) Review the joint actions used in Sun Salutation A and B, focusing on how major joints action of flexion and extension were equally or not equally utilized.
   b) If you wanted to add a few poses to your Sun Salutations to better equalize flexion and extension of spine and hips, what might those poses be?

4. Muscle Actions
   a) Review the muscle actions used in Sun Salutation A and B, focusing on opposing actions. Did any body part receive significantly more contracting than stretching?
   b) If you wanted to add a few poses to your Sun Salutations to better equalize contraction (strengthening) in the lower front body, what might those poses be?

5. Move

Take a class labeled Sun Salutations A and B. Apply the modifications you have practiced for yourself in any pose that is needed. Before and after class, note sensations in the following areas of your body.

> Before: My heart feels ___________, my head feels __________, my feet feel ___________.
> After: My heart feels ___________, my head feels __________, my feet feel ___________.

Standing Series

"Let him that would move the world first move himself" – Socrates.

In the Ashtanga Primary Series, after 5 repetitions each of Sun A and Sun B, the Standing Series begins. Each standing pose is held for 5 Ujjayi breaths, except for in the vinyasa before Warrior I. Standing poses can increase stability, balance, core strength, circulation, coordination, concentration, stamina, and build energy. Important notes for the Ashtanga Primary Standing Series are:

- ✓ When using the Standing Series in Ashtanga, follow the "Ashtanga Primary Series Class" outline.
- ＊ When sequencing these poses in <u>other</u> than the Ashtanga sequence, refer to "Sequence" ideas; and for poses listed that are two-sided poses, repeat on left side.
- ✓ 5-Pointed Star occurs repeatedly as a transition between poses.
- ✓ Cautions presented cannot cover all variables and are not a substitute for medical advice.
- ✓ If a practitioner is without use of one or more limbs, modify variations to engage available joints.
- ✓ Twists/revolved poses: if a practitioner has a spinal injury, is pre-natal, has osteoporosis, etc., staying higher in the twist will better serve spinal integrity. For example, the standing variation of Revolved Side Angle provides similar benefits without weighted revolution of the spine.
- ✓ Forward Bends: if a practitioner has lower back conditions (injury, pregnancy, osteoporosis, SI dysfunction, etc.), reduce the angle of flexion, hold a chair and/or use props for spinal support.
- ✓ Chair variation: practitioners who can stand with stability may research additional sources for using the chair as a prop, rather than a seat, for some poses.
- ✓ Prop variation: Props should be considered in other variations of the Standing Series as blocks or dowels can support muscular strength and spinal integrity. However, using straps in Extended Leg (Utthita Hasta Padangusthasana) is not recommended in an Ashtanga series as set up time for straps detracts from the energetic flow of the series. Instead of straps, utilize a wall for support.
- ✓ For poses previously covered that show up in the Standing Series between Half Bound Lotus and Warrior 2, the same notes on alternating legs in Chair and Reclining variations apply here.
- ✓ An image that depicts variations of all Standing Series poses in one glance is not provided. Review the mixed mobility group class images for Sun A and Sun B and construct a similar one for the Standing Series if you desire.

10. **Big Toe Pose – Padangushtasana** (Pada = foot; Angust = big toe)

Chakras/Doshas/Vayus. Root, 3rd Eye/All except if Kapha or Vata Imbalance/Downward, upward.

Cautions.   Prenatal, back conditions or osteoporosis.

Benefits.   Can increase flexibility in feet, legs, glutes, and spine, and decrease stress.

`Cues.   From Mountain, inhale arms upward and hop feet wide to sides of mat.

Exhale to hinge at waist and bring peace fingers to big toes.

Bend knees to lengthen spine, fingers pull upward as toes press down.

Inhale to look up toward front with straight spine and bent elbows.

Exhale to look back, deepen fold, gently straighten arms and legs.

Sequence.   Hand Under Foot Pose, Mountain.

Variations.   Hands on hips, thighs, or behind back with wider stance.

In chair, sit forward on chair edge, flex feet, and place hands on blocks.

Hands on block to lessen flexion.

Recline and hug knees into chest.

11. **Hand Under Foot Pose - Pada Hastasana** (Pada = Foot; Hasta - Hand)

Chakras/Doshas/Vayus. Root, 3rd Eye/All except if Kapha or Vata Imbalance/Downward, upward.

Cautions.   Prenatal, back conditions or osteoporosis.

Benefits.   Can improve flexibility in hamstrings, calves, shoulders, and spine, and decrease stress.

Cues.   From Big Toe Pose or Forward Bend, inhale and look forward.

Exhale hands under feet with palms up (bend knees as needed).

Draw sit bones upward, gaze at shins.

To come out, inhale look forward, exhale hands to waist, inhale rise.

Sequence.   Hand Under Foot Pose, Mountain, Halfway Lift.

Variations.   Hands on hips, thighs, or behind back with wider stance.

In chair, sit on chair edge, flex feet, and place hands on blocks.

Hands on block to lessen flexion, extend wrists if available

Reclining in Happy Baby Pose with palms over feet.

12. 5-Pointed Star – Utthita Tadasana (Utthita = Extended, Tada = Mountain)

Chakras/Doshas/Vayus. Sacral, Solar Plexus, Heart/All/Balancing, expanding.

Cautions. None.

Benefits. Overall strength, circulation, focus, and self-esteem.

Cues. From Mountain, exhale to step right foot.

Body faces long edge of mat.

Arms extend outward with palms down.

Feet are under palms, navel draws inward.

Lift crown, stabilize shoulders, active arms and fingers.

Sequence. Mountain, Extended and Revolved Triangle.

Variations. Cactus arms and/or lessen width of stance.

Chair Star, knees, and ankles are wide, extend arms.

Blocks in hands for strength or dowel across shoulders.

Recline with legs and arms outward in star shape.

13. Extended Triangle – Utthita Trikonasana (Utthita = extended, tri = three, kona = angle)

Chakras/Doshas/Vayus. Sacral, Solar Plexus, Throat, Heart/All/Downward, balancing, expanding.

Cautions. Props for alignment are recommended.

Benefits. Stretches IT, chest, and neck, and can decrease low back tension.

Cues. From Star, turn right toes to mat short edge, reach right hand forward.

Exhale to lower right hand inside right leg and raise left hand.

Right leg straight; back foot edge presses down.

Shoulders and hips are stacked; gaze is to top thumb.

When both sides complete, inhale back to 5-Pointed Star.

Sequence. 5-Pointed Star. Warrior II, Lizard.

Variations. Top hand on hip, elbow points up, Qigong Side Stretch.

In Chair Star, bring right hand to right side of chair.

Use dowel for alignment or place block under bottom hand.

Recline on left side, extend right leg up (use strap if needed).

14. **Revolved Triangle - Parivrtta Trikonasana** (Parivrtta = Revolved, Tri = Three)

Chakras/Doshas/Vayus. Sacral, Solar, Heart, Throat/All except Vata Imbalance/Downward, balancing.

Cautions. Osteoporosis and pre-natal.

Benefits. Stretches legs and shoulders. Can improve digestion and spinal health.

Cues. From Star, exhale right toes to short edge of mat.

Inhale left arm up and turn torso to face right.

Exhale left hand next to right foot, right hand and gaze extend upward.

Stack shoulders, back foot presses down for stability.

To come out, exhale gaze and shoulders towards floor,

inhale reverse windmill left arm to Star for other side.

Sequence. 5-Pointed Star, Runner's Lunge, Plank.

Variations. Upper hand on waist and lessen angle.

Chair Seated Twist.

Bottom hand on block.

Recline in Reclining Twist.

15. **Extended Side Angle – Utthita Parsvakonasana** (Utthita=extended, Parsva=side, Kona=angle)

Chakras/Doshas/Vayus. Sacral, Solar, Heart, Throat /All/Downward, balancing, expanding.

Cautions. Knee and shoulder conditions.

Benefits. Stretches/strengthens legs and shoulders.

Can improve stamina, digestion, and menses pain.

Cues. From Star, turn right toes to short edge of mat.

Exhale lower right hand as right knee bends over ankle.

Left hand and gaze turn upward as core stabilizes and lifts.

Press back foot down, draw front knee towards little toe.

To come out, inhale to Star, then repeat on other side.

Sequence. Revolved Extended Angle, Bird of Paradise, Lizard.

Variations. Top hand forward over ear, in a bind, or on hip.

In chair, right knee-right side, left leg straight-left side, right arm up.

Block under bottom hand or bottom forearm on thigh.

Reclining Tree with side bend.

16. Revolved Extended Side Angle - **Parivrtta Parsvakonasana** (Parivrtta=Revolved, Parsva=Side, Kona=angle)

Chakras/Doshas/Vayus. All except 3rd Eye or Crown/All except if Vata Imbalance/Downward, balancing.

Cautions. Osteoporosis and pre-natal.

Benefits. Stretches legs and shoulders. Can improve digestion and spinal health.

Cues. From Star, inhale right toes to mat short edge.

Reverse windmill left arm back and upward as torso turns to face right.

Exhale left hand next to right foot, bend right knee above right ankle.

Stack shoulders, right hand, and gaze upward, back foot presses down.

To come out, exhale gaze and shoulders towards floor,

inhale reverse left arm and torso to return to Star.

Sequence. Exhale to Runner's Lunge or Plank.

Variations. Standing Twist or top hand reaches forward over ear.

Sit in chair for Seated Twist.

Block under bottom hand, heel lifts.

Reclining Twist.

Ease Up Mario

Parts of our spines can revolve a lot, like the cervical part (neck), and other parts can revolve moderately, like the thoracic part (mid-back). But when twists (revolved poses) are initiated without preparation, often the part of the spine that gets tasked the most is the one with the least rotation allowance, the lumbar spine (low back). The lumbar spine is meant for foundatonal stability of the torso, so twisting from the lumbar spine promotes disc and sacroiliac joint injury.

When I was learning to drive and kept speeding into and overcorrecting on turns, my Dad compared me to a famous race car driver and told me to stay in my lane until time came to begin turning naturally.

Spinal twists are a lot like a car's steering column that includes a base/gear box (fixed and heavy like the lumbar spine), steering shaft (stable rotation like the thoracic spine) and steering wheel (turns most freely like the cervical spine). If the car's steering base or lumbar spine twist too much, the torque would overcorrect the vehicle under tension and lead to instability in the whole column. Turning safely from the steering shaft or thoracic spine can be done from the middle back if the base/lumbar is solid.

So, add a step before twisting on the exhale. Stabilize by lengthening the spine first (lining up with the pelvis), then twist from your lane (navel area and up), and finish by allowing gaze (neck) to follow. If you or your students haven't figured out what that feels like yet, follow similar cues for Revolved Extended Angle from 5-Pointed Star by using the reverse windmill motion of the back hand – it changes where the twist starts from. Or if your transition into this pose is from another pose, simply line up the pelvis first before hinging forward about 45 degrees, and then engage the twist on an exhale from the navel point.

17. Wide Legged Forward Fold – Prasarita Padottanasana (Pada=foot, Ut=intense, Tan=stretch)

Chakras/Doshas/Vayus. 3rd Eye, Crown/All except if Kapha Imbalance/Downward, upward.

Cautions. Back conditions and pre-natal.

Benefits. Stretches hamstrings, calves, glutes, and lower back.

Can reduce mental and physical tension.

Cues. **Prasarita Padottanasana A**

From Star, exhale hinge forward/down with hands to floor.

Gaze is between legs, neck is relaxed, spine is lengthened.

To come out, inhale engage, exhale hands to waist, inhale to Star.

Prasarita Padottanasana B

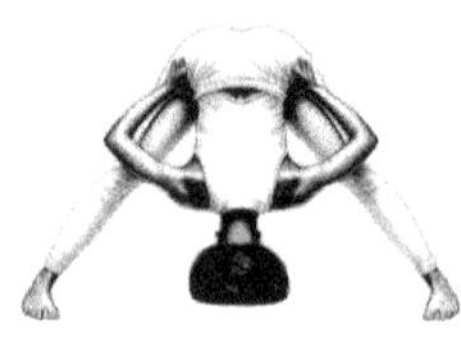

From Star, exhale hinge forward/down with hands to hips.

Gaze is between legs, neck is relaxed, spine is lengthened.

To come out, inhale back to Star.

Prasarita Padottanasana C

From Star, exhale hinge forward/down with hands behind back.

Clasped hands reach towards head (elbows are straight).

Gaze is between legs, neck is relaxed, spine is lengthened.

To come out, inhale back to Star

Prasarita Padottanasana D

From Star, exhale hinge forward/down with peace fingers to big toes

Gaze is between legs, neck is relaxed, spine is lengthened.

To come out, inhale engage, exhale hands to waist, inhale to Star.

Sequence. Half Pyramid, Goddess, Runner's Lunge.

Variations. Legs closer together or Half Lift Variation.

In chair, knee(s) straight and wide to sides, flex toes, and hinge forward.

Hands or head on blocks to maintain length in spine as needed.

Legs Up the Wall, feet wide with strap to support legs as needed.

18. Half Pyramid – Ardha Parsvottanasana (Ardha=Half, Parsva=side or flank, Ut=intense, Tan=stretch)

Chakras/Doshas/Vayus. Root, 3rd Eye/All except if Vata Imbalance/Downward, upward.

Cautions. Prenatal, sacroiliac, and back conditions.

Benefits. Can increase balance and stretch shoulders, wrists, and backs of legs.

Cues. From Mountain, exhale left foot back 1-3'.

Hips and feet face forward, both heels equally weighted.

Inhale to lengthen spine, hands to reverse prayer on back.

Exhale to hinge at waist with flat back.

Crown reaches forward, tailbone back, gaze at big toe.

Other side, inhale lift torso, pivot to face back, exhale into pose.

Sequence. Mountain, Palm Tree, Chair, Runner's Lunge.

Variations. Hands at hips or hands in bind.

Balancing Table with calf stretch (toes on floor).

In Chair, extend one leg, flex toes towards knee, lean into V shape.

Hands on block(s) for back support.

Reclining Hand to Big Toe with strap.

Deep Stability

Yoga poses are not typically the root cause of sacroiliac dysfunction or inflammation, pelvic floor issues, piriformis syndrome, hip bursitis, IT band syndrome, sciatica, hip osteoarthritis, or psoas dysfunction. These pelvic conditions are commonly associated with overuse injuries, prolonged sitting, pregnancy, hormonal changes, trauma, congenital anatomy, age-related cartilage degeneration, or structural misalignments in the pelvis, feet, back, or legs. Often, chronic pelvic conditions can result from combinations of stressors accumulating over time.

However, some yoga poses can contribute to pelvic issues if practiced repeatedly with excessive stretch or tension, and even poses performed with ease can aggravate preexisting pelvic conditions. For example, certain split stances and joint rotations may place excessive demands on ligaments, cartilage, muscles, and tendons, promoting injury or instability. In this book, poses with cautions for pelvic and back conditions offer cues for stability to reduce excessive tension or stretching.

In Pyramid Pose, both legs are straight and split in an open kinetic chain, initiating opposing forces at the sacroiliac joints as the upper body hinges forward to stretch the lower back. For those with pelvic instability, this can trigger painful flareups. Similar benefits can be achieved by bending one or both knees to create a closed-chain action to lessen SI joint stress. Also, poses that engage back muscles while in a split stance such as Warrior III in effect can "brace" against instability by engaging glutes, lower back, and SI joints. While a Warrior III variation does not provide the same back of leg stretch as Pyramid, it does provide related benefits without instability risk for some.

19. Extended Leg – Utthita Hasta Padangusthasana (Utthita=extended, Hasta=hand, Pada=foot, Angusta=big toe)

    Chakras/Doshas/Vayus. Sacral and Solar Plexus/All/Balancing, downward, expanding.

    Cautions. Sacroiliac, shoulder, and lower back conditions.

    Benefits. Can improve balance, strengthen core and strengthen/stretch legs.

    Cues. **Utthita Hasta Padangusthasana A**

    From Mountain, left hand on hip, raise right knee.

    Right fingers grasp right big toe; exhale straighten leg with upright spine.

    Draw hips to midline, gaze forward.

    Utthita Hasta Padangusthasana B

    From A, inhale lengthen spine, exhale open right leg to right side.

    Draw hips to midline, gaze to left side.

    Utthita Hasta Padangusthasana D (C is skipped)

    From B, inhale right leg back to front, hands to waist or sides,

    Lower leg to about 6-12" above ground (modified D version).

    Draw hips to midline, gaze forward.

    Sequence. Mountain, Dancer, Cresent Lunge.

    Variations. Keep right knee bent with hand to inside right knee.

    In chair with strap around right foot toe bases, hold with right hand.

    Stabilize lifted leg, extend right arm for balance.

    Recline in Hand to Big Toe.

"Nobody Puts Baby in the Corner" – Patrick Swayze.

While yoga asana is not a competition, neither is it a spectator sport. Asana requires active engagement in many poses. Physical engagement allows our natural design features (musculoskeletal components, energy movement, nervous system, and endocrine functions, etc.) to collaborate for our wellness. However, people may show up at yoga class pre-conditioned to try not to be seen and/or expect not to be successful, often resulting in a lack of engagement that shows up like "hanging out" in one's bones and joints. Yoga class is one place to practice active engagement in stances that reflect an "I matter" posture that transcends off the mat.

Using support can also lead to optimum engagement. For example, in Utthita Hasta Padangusthasana B, using a block, chair or wall can offer stability for full engagement in a beneficial way. On the flip side, too much support can take away from engagement. Using shoulder and back muscles to torque on a strap to keep your leg lifted in this same pose creates tension in some body parts and disengages other body parts, effectively reducing benefits. In balancing poses, one can practice re-wiring conditioned thoughts and actions to stand confidently engaged in what serves your most meaningful life.

20. Half Bound Lotus (Utthita =extended, Hasta = hand, Pada = foot, Angusta = big toe)

Chakras/Doshas/Vayus. Sacral, 3rd Eye/All except Pitta-Vata Imbalance/Downward, balancing, upward.

Cautions.   Prenatal, knee, ankle, hip, and back conditions.

Benefits.   Strengthens standing leg and stretches muscles in bent leg.

Can improve balance and focus.

Cues.   From Mountain, place left foot on front of pelvis towards right side.

Left hand reaches behind to hold right big toe.

Inhale to raise right hand and lengthen spine.

Hip points and shoulders are "squared" to front, micro bend knees.

Exhale to hinge forward at waist with gaze toward knees.

To come out, inhale torso up, exhale Mountain and do other side.

Sequence.   Chair, Dancer, Cresent Lunge, Palm Tree.

Variations.   Chair pose with right foot on left thigh.

Chair modified Reclining Pigeon.

Block under lower hand for stability when folding.

Recline in Reverse Pigeon.

"No one saves us but ourselves" — Gautama Buddha

Certain poses in the Ashtanga Primary Series were practiced by young Indian men and boys whose lifestyles included outdoor work for a hundred years before these poses were let loose on a global aging population more sedentary in the name of productivity. Some of these same poses continue to be sequenced into group classes comprised of wide varieties of ages and modern bodies. Losing mobility due to an injury that requires rest, ice, and elevation for days, weeks or months, or medical intervention is never something desired, yet many practitioners and yoga teachers tempt fate regularly.

Poses that ask for extensive rotation in knees and hips, such as Pigeon and Half-Bound Lotus, can feel amazing until they don't. While our hips have a wide range of normal rotation, if hip rotation is forced and/or loaded (i.e., leaning forward while hip is adducted or abducted) degradation in joint tissues can occur. Additionally, knee rotation ranges are less than hip ranges, so if knees try to fit into a shape beyond their normal range, then knee tissues risk injury. For example, in Half Bound Lotus, less weighted rotation of knees and hips is often more beneficial, especially for Vatas and Pittas. And Pigeon is not included in this book as the weighting of a rotated knee by the torso, combined with uneven SI joints, is not conducive to ligament and joint integrity for many bodies. Limiting practice of poses that call for joint actions beyond normal ranges and adding more stabilizing poses into practice can increase wellness over a longer period. In the present moment, you always have a choice . . . and each choice and action related to that choice informs what comes next.

21. Warrior II – Virabhadrasana II (Virabhadra = mythical Hindu God)

    Chakras/Doshas/Vayus. Solar Plexus, Heart/All/Balancing, downward, expanding.

    Cautions. Knee and shoulder conditions.

    Benefits. Stretches hips, groin, and chest.
    Strengthens legs, torso, and arms.
    Can increase stamina and circulation.

    Cues. Exhale back foot parallel to short edge of mat (90 degrees).
    Extend arms outward (hands above feet) with palms down.
    Left knee bends and aligns over left ankle.
    Outer edge of back foot presses downward,
    Shoulders draw down, navel engages toward spine
    Head aligns over tailbone, gaze across front middle finger.

    Sequence. Reverse Warrior, Plank, Extended Side Angle, Star, Runner's Lunge.

    Variations. Lessen width and depth of stance, or Kneeling Warrior II.
    In chair, bend right knee over right side, left leg extends to left side, extend arms.
    Dowel across shoulders for engagement and alignment.
    Reclining Prone Warrior II (image is view from under floor), face rests on hand in Archer.

The Ripple Effect

Actions create a ripple effect of energy that grows like a drop in water expanding outward. This principle of energy in motion means that every pose engagement, alignment, and transition can have exponential benefits. For example, Warrior II can feel nice, or it can feel like waves of energy within your body; and coming into or out of Warrior II can feel like routine steps, or it can feel like energy collaborating towards expansion. The difference is in the somatic experience.

Try Warrior II using the cues above for alignment, then bring attention to fully engaging your feet. Once you've established that energy, you may notice that energy rise up your calves, shins, knees, and thighs. Take that uplifting energy and expand it across your hips, up through your torso and across arms to active fingertips before that expansion returns to center and effortlessly lifts your spine upward. Transitions are also opportunities to continue expansion through physical tissues and subtle energy.

The Ashtanga Primary sequence cues Warrior II from Warrior I in a way that can promote pelvic, hip and knee muscle, ligament, and tendon issues. Since stable hip, knee and ankle rotation in Warrior I differ from Warrior II, transition between the two creates an unnatural shift as the extended limb attempts movement meant to originate from the hips. Instead of interrupting energy, try cartwheeling hands on the exhale from Warrior I to Runner's Lunge, then inhaling to Crescent Lunge and exhaling to Warrior II to stay in an unbroken somatic experience that can expand energy further.

22. Crow Pose – Bakasana (Baka=Crow or Crane)

Chakras/Doshas/Vayus. Throat, 3rd Eye/All except if Pitta Imbalance/Upward, downward, balancing.

Cautions. Pre-natal, back, shoulder and wrist conditions.

Benefits. Can strengthen arms and core while improving coordination.

Cues. From Forward Bend, place hands shoulder-width apart on mat.
Fingers wide, knuckles press downward for upward stability.
Bend elbows, heel toe feet wider than hands.
Place shins on forearms so knees are near armpits.
Gaze forward of hands, lift balls of feet and lean forward.
Apply Uddiyana bandh, straighten arms, press tailbone toward heels.
Lift feet up and draw heels to buttocks; big toes come together.

Sequence. Plank, Squat, Easy Pose.

Variations. Keep elbows bent for support, or practice Crow prep with toes on floor.
In Chair, bend knees and forward bend to blocks with engagement cues above.
Block under feet and blanket or block under forehead.
Recline with knees into chest, press knees into forearms as hands reach upward.

Where Focus Goes, Energy Follows

If you have done single track mountain biking, trail running, or horseback riding, you know that if you get scared and look down at wheels or feet, the rest of you is more likely to go down too. Often, the key to staying upright in balancing yoga asanas is what you set your sights on.

Looking ahead typically provides the nervous system input needed to relay messages to your body as to what voluntary and autonomic responses are necessary. For example, in Crow pose, with proper set-up and practice, balance is easier to achieve when the gaze is forward. Our bodies and minds are genius, so small yogic hacks like drishti (eye gaze) go a long way in providing focus to elevate benefits of your practice.

In the traditional Ashtanga Primary Series, modified crow pose – sometimes extended into handstand - is used to initiate chaturanga (Plank to Upward Facing Dog to Downward Facing Dog). Here it is added at the end of the Standing Series, rather than later in the series, to offer a transition between standing poses and seated poses. New awareness only and always leads to new opportunity.

Standing Series Actions

Pose	Spine	Shoulders	Hips	Knees	Upper Front Contracts	Upper Front Stretches	Upper Back Contracts	Upper Back Stretches	Lower Front Contracts	Lower Front Stretches	Lower Back Contracts	Lower Back Stretches	Side Body Adduction	Side Body Abduction
Ujjayi Breath	Neutral	Rotation	Neutral	Neutral	No	No	No	No	No	No	No	No	No	No
Big Toe	Flexion	Flexion	Flexion	Neutral	Yes	No	No	Yes	Yes	No	No	Yes	No	No
Hand Under Foot	Flexion	Flexion	Flexion	Neutral	Yes	No	No	Yes	Yes	No	No	Yes	No	No
5-Pointed Star	Extension	Abduction	Abduction	Extension	No	Yes	No	Yes	No	No	No	No	No	Yes
Extended Triangle	Extension	Extension	Rot/Abd	Extension	No	Yes	No	Yes	Yes	Yes	No	Yes	No	Yes
Revolved Triangle	Rotation	Extension	Rot/Abd	Extension	Yes	Yes	No	Yes	Yes	Yes	No	Yes	No	Yes
Ext Side Angle	Extension	Extension	Flex/Rot/Abd	Flex/Ext	No	Yes	No	Yes	Yes	Yes	No	Yes	No	Yes
Rev Side Angle	Rotation	Extension	Flex/Rot/Abd	Flex/Ext	Yes	Yes	No	Yes	Yes	Yes	No	Yes	No	Yes
Wide Leg FF A	Flexion	Flexion	Flex/Rot/Abd	Extension	Yes	No	No	Yes	Yes	No	No	Yes	No	Yes
Wide Leg FF B	Flexion	Flexion	Flex/Rot/Abd	Extension	Yes	No	No	Yes	Yes	No	No	Yes	No	Yes
Wide Leg FF C	Flexion	Ext/Add	Flex/Rot/Abd	Extension	Yes	No	No	Yes	Yes	No	No	Yes	No	Yes
Wide Leg FF D	Flexion	Flexion	Flex/Rot/Abd	Extension	Yes	No	No	Yes	Yes	No	No	Yes	No	Yes
Pyramid	Flexion	Ext/Add	Flex/Ext	Extension	Yes	No	No	Yes	Yes	No	No	Yes	No	No
Leg Extended A	Extension	Flexion	Flexion	Extension	No	No	No	No	Yes	No	No	Yes	No	No
Leg Extended B	Extension	Abduction	Flex/Rot/Abd	Extension	No	No	No	No	No	Yes	No	Yes	No	Yes
Leg Extended C	Extension	Flexion	Flexion	Extension	No	No	No	No	Yes	No	No	No	No	No
Half Bound Lotus	Flexion	Flexion	Add/Rot	Flex/Ext	Yes	No	No	Yes	Yes	Yes	No	Yes	Yes	No
Chair	Flexion	Flex/Rot	Flexion	Flexion	No	Yes	No	Yes	Yes	No	Yes	No	No	No
Forward Bend	Flexion	Flexion	Flexion	Neutral	Yes	No	No	Yes	Yes	No	No	Yes	No	No
Halfway Lift	Extension	Flexion	Flexion	Neutral	Yes	No	Yes	No	Yes	No	No	No	No	No
Plank	Neutral	Flexion	Neutral	Neutral	Yes	No	Yes	No	Yes	No	Yes	No	No	No
Mid-Plank	Neutral	Extension	Neutral	Neutral	Yes	No	Yes	No	Yes	No	Yes	No	No	No
Upward Dog	Extension	Extension	Extension	Neutral	No	Yes	Yes	No	No	Yes	Yes	No	No	No
Cobra	Extension	Extension	Neutral	Neutral	No	Yes	Yes	No	No	No	No	No	No	No
Down Dog	Neutral	Flex/Rot	Flexion	Neutral	No	Yes	No	Yes	Yes	Yes	Yes	Yes	No	Yes
Warrior I	Extension	Flex/Rot	Flex/Ext/Rot	Flex/Rot Ext	No	Yes	No	Yes	Yes	Yes	Yes	Yes	No	Yes
Warrior 2	Extension	Abduction	Flexion	Flex/Ext	No	Yes	No	Yes	Yes	Yes	No	Yes	No	Yes
Crow	Flexion	Flexion	Flexion	Flexion	Yes	No	Yes	No	Yes	No	Yes	No	No	No
# Flexion	10	14	19	7										
# Extension	11	9	3	15										
# Rotation	2	4	11	1										
# Abduction		3	9											
# Adduction		2	1											
TOTAL # YES					15	12	6	18	23	10	7	18	1	13

Actions do not include those used for structure under typical load or in transition to/from pose.

Primary actions may be multiple (i.e., when legs or arms in differing directions from such as Warrior I).

Practice

1. Breathe

    Review Sitali and Caliber for Constant Authority in Pranayama. Practice each breath for 3 minutes. Ask someone to let you practice guiding these breaths. Try teaching without notes to integrate more.

2. Teach

    Review the Standing Series poses. Practice each version of the Standing Series a few times using the breath, cue and prop recommendation provided. Then lead someone else through 2 variations of the Standing Series with minimal demonstration and without notes. If your volunteer cannot do all poses and transitions with ease, offer pose variations.

    Then ask your volunteer for feedback in the following areas:

    > What did they see during class?
    >
    > What did they hear during class?
    >
    > What did they feel during class?
    >
    > What was their overall experience of class?
    >
    > What did they like best about your teaching?
    >
    > What is one thing they could tell you to help you grow?

3. Joint Actions
    a) Review the joint actions used in the Standing Series, focusing on how major joints action of flexion and extension were equally or not equally utilized.
    b) If you wanted to add a few poses to the Standing Series to better equalize flexion and extension of the hips, what might those poses be?

4. Muscle Actions
    a) Review the muscle actions used in Standing Series, focusing on opposing actions. Did any body part receive significantly more contracting than stretching?
    b) If you wanted to add a few poses to your Standing Series to better equalize contraction (strengthening) in the lower back body, what might those poses be?

5. Move

    Take a class labeled Ashtanga Vinyasa Primary Standing Series. Before and after class, note sensations in the following areas of your body.

    > Before: My heart feels ___________, my head feels _________, my feet feel ___________.
    >
    > After: My heart feels ___________, my head feels _________, my feet feel ___________.

Seated Series

"Nothing can bring you peace but yourself" — *Ralph Waldo Emerson.*

In the Ashtanga Primary Series, after 5 repetitions each of Sun A and Sun B, and then longer holds in Standing Series poses, the Seated Series begins. Seated poses are held for 5 breaths (equal counts) while transitional poses from and to these seated poses are breath to movement. At this point in the Ashtanga sequence, the Seated Series draws attention and energy toward inner peace through a sort of resilience calibration. Important notes for this Ashtanga Seated Series are:

- ✓ When using the Standing Series in Ashtanga, follow the "Ashtanga Primary Series Class" outline.
- * When sequencing these poses in <u>other</u> than the Ashtanga preset sequence, refer to "Sequence" ideas; and for poses listed that are two-sided poses, repeat on left side.
- ✓ Cautions presented cannot cover all variables and are not a substitute for medical advice.
- ✓ If a practitioner is without use of one or more limbs, modify variations to engage available joints.
- ✓ Some poses in the Primary Ashtanga Seated Series are not included here as they may not contribute to overall functional wellness for many practitioners.
- ✓ In the Chair, Prop and Reclining versions, performing transitions is not recommended to allow time for adjustment of body and props.
- ✓ Gentle variation: the transitional pose of Deer should alternate which leg is in front; if getting up and down from the floor is not an option, a chair, bed, or massage table works just as well.
- ✓ Forward Bends: if a practitioner has lower back conditions (injury, pregnancy, osteoporosis, SI dysfunction, etc.), use pose variations, reduce the angle of flexion, and/or use props such as a folded blanket under tailbone, a rolled blanket under knees, and blocks under hands for alignment.
- ✓ Transitions in the Seated Series occur between each side of 2-sided seated poses, except that practitioners can always choose to skip the transition and stay seated to prepare for next pose. The less sound your body makes in transition, the more stability that is present. See the image depicting two variations of transition poses (regular and gentle) on the next page.
- ✓ An image that depicts variations of all Seated Series poses in one glance is not provided. Review the mixed mobility group class images for Sun A and Sun B and construct a similar one for the Seated Series if you desire.

23. Transition to and from Seated

Chakras/Doshas/Vayus. Solar Plexus, 3rd Eye/All except Pitta or Vata Imbalance/Balancing, expanding.

Cautions. Shoulders, wrist, feet, and back conditions.

Hopping through without ease and control increases risk of injury to joints.

Benefits. Can strengthen entire body and increase focus.

Overall. Transitions in the Seated Series occur between each seated pose and each side of 2-sided seated poses. Movement is silent, smooth, and steady.

Cues for A. For transition from Downward Dog TO Seated, inhale bend knees and come up on toes.

Engage Mula and Uddiyana bandhas to lift legs into core, look forward.

Exhale to "fly" legs through arms and land quietly in Staff Pose.

From Staff, do the next seated pose in series.

For transition FROM any seated pose, inhale to cross legs.

Exhale hands in front of knees and press legs back to Plank.

Variations. Skip the transition and stay seated to prepare for next pose.

Cues for B. From Down Dog, come to Table, then Deer, Easy Pose, and lastly lengthen legs to Staff.

From Staff, come to Deer, then Table and Cow, and lastly to Downward Dog.

24. Seated Straight Legged/Staff – Dandasana (Danda = Staff)

Chakras/Doshas/Vayus. Root, Solar Plexus/All/Downward, balancing.

Cautions.   Back conditions.

Benefits.   Can reduce back, hamstring, and mental tension.

Cues.   Extend legs long with micro bend in knees.

Place hands on floor near hips, palms down, fingers forward.

Press hands and backs of legs downward.

Flex feet, reach through heels.

Broaden chest, draw navel inward, lift crown, gaze forward.

Sequence.   Forward Fold A/B, Bound Angle, Reverse Plank/Table.

Variations. Bend knees slightly, hands behind back for support.

Sit forward on chair, extend legs, heels down, flex feet.

Sit forward on bolster to raise tailbone.

Legs Up the Wall with back, arms pressing downward.

Engaged Relaxation

Staff Pose requires muscular engagement and focus, asking us to sit still without relaxing or planning our next move. All of this can offer a surprising feeling of mind-body control. But what comes after Seated Staff pose in Ashtanga's Seated Series sequence are seated folds that call for safe relenting of effort.

Yoga teachers often offer seated folds in group classes of mixed ages, genders, body types, and health conditions. However, in seated forward folding postures, lower limbs are stationery and the primary stretch is in the spine and its supporting muscles. Since many people sit and lean forward much of their day, this spinal flexion is not lacking in daily life – in fact, it is often done excessively.

Using props in seated folds/bends helps preserve spinal integrity while allowing relaxation. For example, raising the tailbone by sitting forward on a folded blanket creates a more stable base from which the spine can hinge forward from – resulting in less rounding of the back. Similarly, placing a narrowly rolled blanket under the knees reduces gravitational pull of tight hamstrings, so the spine is not forced to compensate.

While seated folds/bends can be a welcome part of practice, too many bends/folds can undermine long-term stability. Over time, repeated forward folding can contribute to ligament laxity, muscular imbalance, and chronic back pain.

25. Seated Forward Fold A and B - Paschimattanasana (Paschima=west, Ut=intense, Tan=to stretch)

Chakras/Doshas/Vayus. Root, 3rd Eye/All except Vata Imbalance/Downward.

Cautions. Pre-natal, back conditions, and practitioners who round backs.

Benefits. Stretches back body and can ease tension.

Cues. **Seated Forward Fold A**

From Staff, inhale arms upward to lengthen spine.

Exhale to hinge forward, peace fingers to big toes.

Chest toward thighs; knees bent to maintain spine length.

Inhale look up and lengthen spine, exhale fold deeper.

Seated Forward Fold B

From A, move hands to bottoms of feet.

Inhale look up and lengthen spine, exhale fold deeper.

To come out, inhale to lengthen, exhale hands back to Staff.

Sequence. Staff, Head to Knee Pose, Bound Angle.

Variations. Widen legs, bend knees, and bring hands to shins instead of feet.

In chair, sit on edge to perform cues above.

Place blocks under hands, sit forward on bolster with padding under knees.

Reclining knees into chest.

26. Reverse Plank – Purvatanasana (Purva = east, Ut = intense, Tan = stretch)

Chakras/Doshas/Vayus. Solar Plexus, Heart, Throat/All/Inward, balancing, upward.

Cautions. Pre-natal, shoulder, wrist, and neck conditions.

Benefits. Strengthens and stretches whole body; can improve energy and focus.

Cues. From Staff, place hands behind hips 2-5"

Fingers point to toes, hands and fingers press down.

Chest lifts with spine, upper arms rotate outward.

Press soles of feet down, legs are straight and firm.

Chin shift slightly upward to open throat.

Sequence. Staff, Head to Knee Pose, Happy Baby.

Variations. Reverse Table (lessen lift if prenatal or wrist concerns).

Sit on chair edge, hands on sides, straighten legs, lift hips.

Recline, neck and forearms on mat, press into flexed heels and forearms to lift torso/legs.

   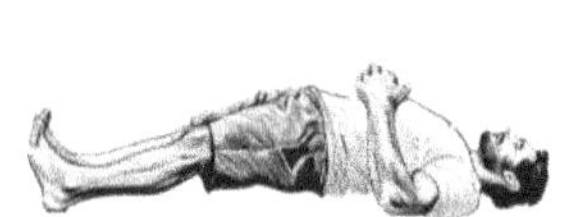

27. **Head to Knee Pose - Janu Shirshasana A** (Janu=knee, Sirsa=head)

Chakras/Doshas/Vayus. Root, Sacral, 3rd Eye/All except Vata Imbalance/Downward.

Cautions. Pre-natal, hip, back and shoulder conditions.

Benefits. Stretches back body and can ease tension.

Cues. From Staff, place left foot inside of right thigh.

Inhale arms up, lengthen spine, square torso front.

Exhale, hinge forward as hands reach around foot.

Chest toward thigh; knee bent to maintain length in spine.

Inhale gaze up to lengthen spine, exhale hinge deeper.

To go to other side, inhale gaze up and forward, then exhale hands to Staff.

Sequence. Sage Tree, Easy Pose, Bound Angle, Reclining Tree.

Variations. Bring hands to shins instead of feet.

In chair, straighten left knee, rotate right hip to right side, flex right toes, hinge forward.

Sit forward on bolster, place block under long leg and padding under knee.

Reclining Tree.

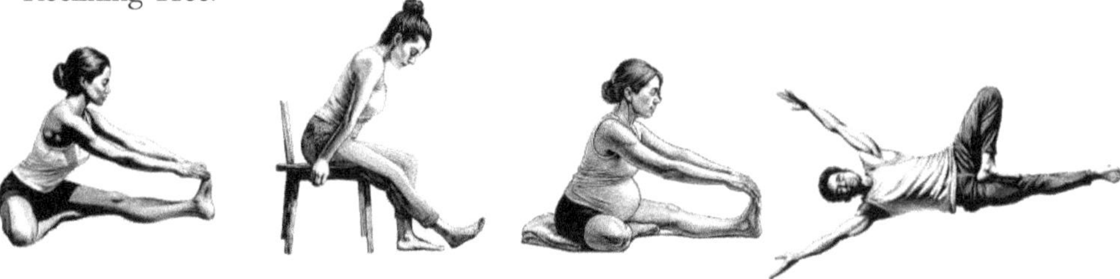

28. **Sage Twist – Marichyasana C** (Pose for Sage Marichi)

Chakras/Doshas/Vayus. Root, Throat, 3rd Eye/All except Vata Imbalance/Downward, balancing.

Cautions. Pre-natal, sacroiliac, osteoporosis, and low back conditions.

Benefits. Can improve digestion, spinal flexibility, and clarity.

Cues. From Staff, place left foot next to upper right thigh, flex right foot.

Inhale both arms up to lengthen spine, exhale cactus arms.

Rotate middle back to bring left upper arm outside of right. knee.

Left forearm reaches behind knee to meet right arm behind back.

Lengthen spine, press sit bones downward, gaze right.

To come out, inhale arms up, exhale to back to start.

Sequence. Boat, Easy Pose, Bound Angle.

Variations. Right hand on floor, left elbow inside left knee, lessen angle of knee to reduce rotation.

Chair Seated Twist.

Sit forward on bolster to raise tailbone, padding under long knees, then rotate into twist.

Reclining Twist.

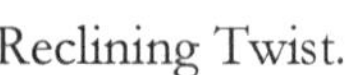

29. Boat Pose – Paripurna Navasana (Paripurna=complete, nava=boat)

Chakras/Doshas/Vayus. Solar Plexus/All except Pitta Imbalance/Balancing, expanding.

Cautions. Pre-natal and back conditions. Repetitive flexed psoas loading can lead to back instability.

Benefits. Can strengthen entire front body and stimulate endocrine system.

Cues. From Staff, bend knees to lean backward on sit bones and tailbone.
Lengthen front torso and inhale lift feet to straighten legs.
Arms stretch along body and reach through fingers.
Broaden shoulders, gaze toward toes with neutral neck.

Sequence. Bound Angle, Bridge or Fish.

Variations. Keep feet on mat, hands on legs, lean backward to engage.
Sit near chair edge, lift feet, and lean upper torso backward.
Place hands on dowel behind back, lean back with control.
Stretch Pose, place blanket under head and feet if desired.

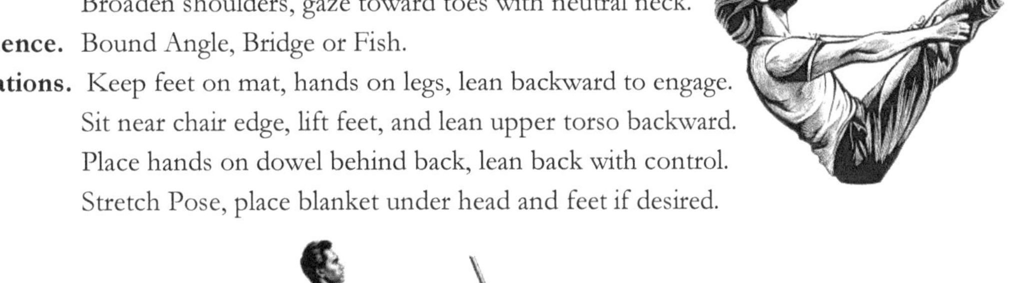

30. Bound Angle - Baddha Konasana (Baddha = Bound, Kona = Angel)

Chakras/Doshas/Vayus. Root, Sacral/All/Downward.

Cautions. Knee conditions.

Benefits. Stretches inner thighs, groins and knees; can reduce pelvic tension.

Cues. From Staff, bring soles of feet together with knees out to sides.
Place hands on feet, hinge forward at hips, gaze at floor.
To go further, bring head to rest on floor.
To come out, inhale walk hands back to return to upright spine.

Sequence. Bridge, Deer, Reclining Bound Angle.

Variations. Sit with knees higher and not as wide.
Sit in chair with legs open to sides, rest feet on stool.
Recline in Reclining Bound Angle, or in Legs Up Wall variation.
Recline in Restorative Bound Angle using a narrow, long bolster placed on 2 blocks at varying height to support the spine lengthwise. Place props under knees and arms.

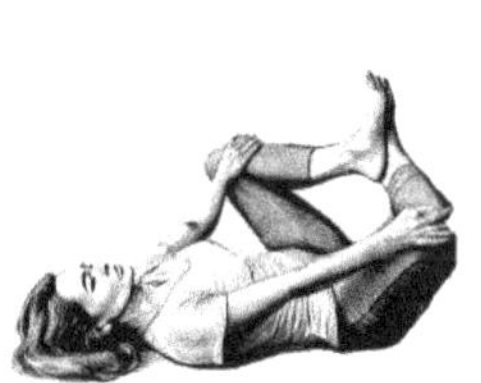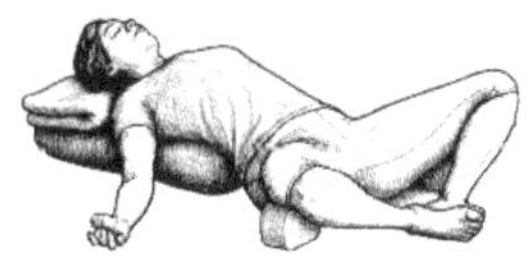

Finishing Series

The soul says I'm ok, I've never not been.

The Ashtanga Primary Series finishes with Finishing Series that are each held for 5-10 breaths (not Ujjayi). By this point in the Ashtanga sequence, Sun Salutations A and B have already helped to energize the mind and body, even out fascia, lubricate joints, increase flexibility and strength; the Standing Series has supported increased stability, balance, core strength, coordination, stamina and focus; the Seated Series drew attention and energy inward; and now the Finishing Series supports the practitioner's tuning into sustained single-pointed focus, or the practice of Dharana. All of this has been in preparation for the series final pose, Savasana, where mind is liberated in space and time. Important notes for this Ashtanga Finishing Series:

- ✓ Transitions used in the Seated series are NOT used in the Finishing Series.
- ✓ When using the Seated Series in Ashtanga, follow the "Ashtanga Primary Series Class" outline.
- * When sequencing these poses in <u>other</u> than the Ashtanga sequence, refer to "Sequence" ideas.
- ✓ Cautions presented cannot cover all variables and are not a substitute for medical advice.
- ✓ If a practitioner is without use of one or more limbs, modify variations to engage available joints.
- ✓ Many poses in the Finishing portion of the Ashtanga Primary series are not included here as they pose injury risks that can be difficult to mitigate.
- ✓ For all variations: poses are shown on the floor. If a practitioner cannot get on and off the floor, a bed or massage/ therapy table works just as well.
- ✓ Come out of inversions slowly, methodically and with control – don't wait until tired.
- ✓ Forward Bends: if a practitioner has lower back conditions (injury, pregnancy, osteoporosis, SI dysfunction, etc.), use variations, reduce the angle of flexion, and/or use props such as a folded blanket under the tailbone, a rolled blanket under knees, and blocks under hands for alignment.
- ✓ An image that depicts variations of all Finishing Series poses in one glance is not provided. Review the mixed mobility group class images for Sun A and Sun B and construct a similar one for the Finishing Series if you desire.

31. Bridge - Setu Bandhasana Sarvangasana (Setu = bridge, Banha = lock, Sarva=all, Anga = limb)

Chakras/Doshas/Vayus. Solar, Heart, Throat/All/Inward, upward, downward, balancing.

Cautions.	Blood pressure or vertigo conditions.
Benefits.	Stretches spine and hip flexors, strengthens legs, can stabilize pelvis while reducing stress.
Cues.	On back with knees bent, walk feet towards glutes to align knees, hips, and ankles.
	Extend arms along body, palms down; feet and arms press down.
	Lift hips up, engage glutes and legs.
	Clasp hands under body (forearms/knuckles press down).
	To come out, release torso back to the floor.
Sequence.	Wheel, Happy Baby, Spinal Twist.
Variations.	Lessen hip lift, hands remain in start position.
	Squeeze block/ball for pelvic floor engagement.
	Block under sacrum (extend legs for psoas stretch).
	Prone side Bow, bend one knee at time or place block under sacrum.

32. Wheel - Urdhva Dhanurasana (Urdva = Upward, Dhanu = bow, or Chakra = wheel)

Chakras/Doshas/Vayus. Solar, Heart, Throat/All except imbalances/Inward, balancing, upward, expanding.

Cautions.	Pre-natal, neck, eye, back, shoulder, heart conditions. ALL - do not weight head.
Benefits.	Stretches front body and strengthens arms and legs.
	Can stimulate endocrine system and improve mood.
Cues.	From Bridge set up, bend elbows.
	Place palms at sides of head near shoulders.
	Fingers point to heels; elbows point to ceiling.
	Press into feet, glutes lift.
	Press into hands, shoulders lift.
	Torso rises, thighs slightly inward, gaze to back.
	To come out, release in opposite manner
Sequence.	Shoulder Stand, Happy Baby, or hug knees into chest.
Variations.	Bridge.
	Squat with large exercise behind back, lean back and slowly form wheel pose over ball.
	Prone side or Side Bow.

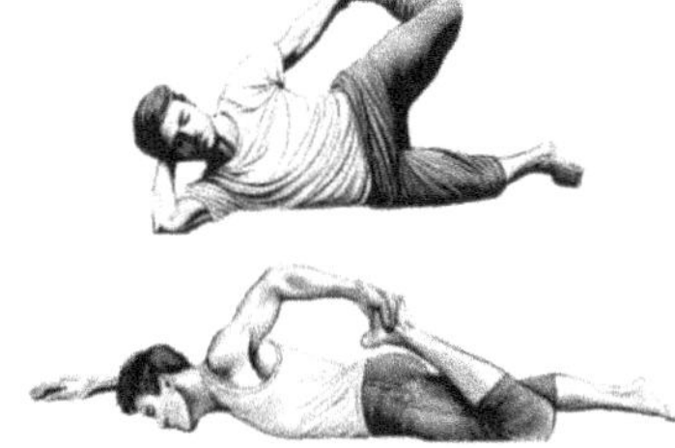

33. Shoulder Stand – Salamba Sarvangasana (Sa = with, Alamba = support, Sarva = all, Anga = limb)

Chakras/Doshas/Vayus. Throat, 3rd Eye/All except Vata-Pitta Imbalance/Inward, upward, balancing.

Cautions.	Stroke risk for all. Pre-natal, neck, eye, and heart conditions.
	Do NOT swing legs up/down or turn head.
	Lessen angle of compression with blanket (allow for back of head to rest on ground).
Benefits.	Stretches neck, strengthens legs/core; stimulates endocrine system and promotes clarity.
Cues.	Lay on back and place folded blanket under torso only (top edge under shoulders).
	Knees are bent with feet on floor, inhale to curl torso inward, knees toward face.
	Bend elbows, hands on lower back, fingers point to ceiling, elbows are parallel.
	Lift thighs with knees bent, then straighten legs and lift through balls of feet.
	Head is aligned with spine, throat is soft, allow space between chin and chest.
	Draw shoulder blades into upper back, gaze is upward.
	To come out, reverse the process slowly and with control.
Sequence.	Child's Pose or Puppy.
Variations.	Legs Up the Wall or extend legs straight upward without the wall.
	Recline with sacrum on a block or bolster.
	Modified Bridge with one leg lifted (alternate legs).

   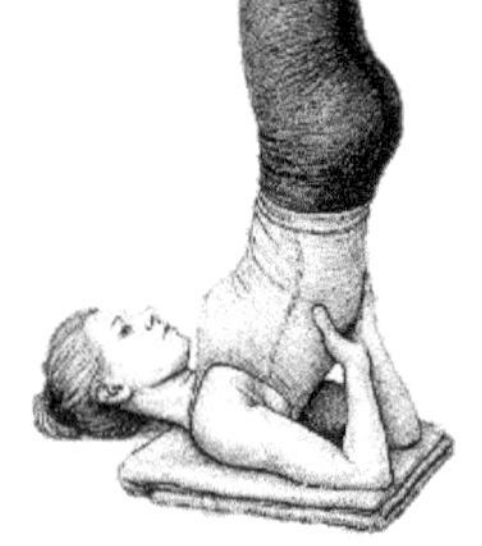

You've Got Some Nerve

Most yoga students and many yoga teachers are unaware that extreme neck flexion and excessive neck loading (such as in unsupported Shoulder Stand, Plow, and Headstands) can harm their cervical spine. I was also unaware of this issue in my 200-hour teacher training. So when a student asked me about the risks of inversions, I admitted ignorance and started researching the answer. I discovered an alarming number of reports of neck injuries in yoga.

Nerve roots and arteries in your neck need safe pathways to the rest of your body for neurological processes, clear vision, good circulation, upper torso stability, and more.. There is enough space for these important nerves and arteries during normal neck flexion ranges (about 40-60 degrees), such as when you tuck your chin to look down. However, when you flex your neck to the end range and place load on that flexion, such as in Shoulder Stand, the force on nerve roots and arteries can create a shearing effect. The result can be acute or chronic tension in sternocleidomastoid and trapezius muscles, aneurysms, vertigo, and glaucoma, strokes, and more.

I went through a period when I stopped teaching Shoulderstand. But with time I realized that my fear was based on learning what not to do – instead of what to do instead. Further research revealed safe ways to experience the benefits of these poses by preparing for safe cues, props, support, and control.

34. Plow – Halasana (Hala=Plow)

Chakras/Doshas/Vayus. Throat, 3rd Eye/All except Vata Imbalance/Inward, upward, downward, balancing

Cautions.   Stroke risk for all. Pre-natal, neck, eye, and heart conditions.

Do NOT swing legs up/down or turn head.

Lessen angle for compression with blanket (allow for back of head to rest on ground).

Benefits.   Stretches neck, strengthens legs/core; stimulates endocrine system and promote clarity.

Cues.   From Should Stand, keep legs straight, hands support back, head aligns with spine.

Slowly lower feet above head, hips over shoulders.

Draw shoulder blades and pelvis inward, arms come down for balance.

Soften throat and space between chin and chest, gaze up.

Option - Ear Pressure pose (bend knees to hug knees to ears).

To come out, reverse the process slowly and with control.

Sequence.   Puppy, Child's Pose, Savasana.

Variations.   Hug knees in toward chest, lift head and slightly tuck chin.

Bring feet to chair seat to lessen angle of back to neck.

Lay on back with legs elevated (pillow under head if desired).

 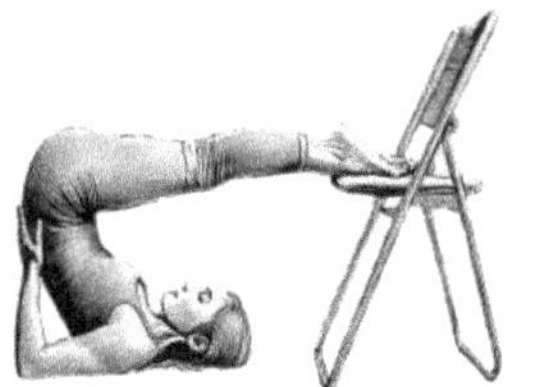 

35. Fish – Matsyasana (Matsya=fish)

Chakras/Doshas/Vayus. Heart, Throat, 3rd Eye/All/Inward, downward, upward, balancing.

Cautions.   Pre-natal, neck, eye, back and heart conditions.

Benefits.   Stretches neck, shoulders, and chest.

Can stimulate endocrine system and promote clarity.

Cues.   From Staff, lean back on bent elbows hugged into torso.

Place hands under hips with palms face down.

Back of pelvis, legs and elbows press downward.

Lift torso as top of head leans toward back.

To come out, softly tuck chin toward chest and widen elbows until spine is neutral/long.

Sequence.   Dolphin, Child's Pose, Puppy, Savasana.

Variations.   Lean back on elbows and slightly lift chin.

Block at highest level under upper back and block on lower level under back of head.

Pace a narrow bolster (or rolled blanket) under lower shoulder girdle.

36. **Dolphin – Ardha Pincha Mayurasana** (Half Feathered Peacock)

Chakras/Doshas/Vayus. Root, 3rd Eye/All except Pitta Imbalance/Downward, upward, balancing.

Cautions.	Pre-natal, shoulder, arm, heart, eye, or prenatal conditions.
Benefits.	Strengthens shoulders, arms, core, and legs. Can reduce headaches, fatigue, tension.
Cues.	From Table, lower elbows to floor beneath shoulders.
	Clasp fingers and place pinky fingers parallel on floor.
	Place back of head in front of cupped hands.
	Distribute weight across forearms and hands, do NOT press top of head into floor.
	Tuck toes, lift knees, legs straighten as pelvis lifts upward.
	Spine is long, shoulders are broad, gaze between legs to navel.
	Align ears with upper arms, lengthen and soften neck muscles.
	Walk feet closer to elbows as body forms the shape of an "A."
	To come out, exhale knees down and return to Table.
	To continue sequence, exhale to Child's Pose.
Sequence.	Supported Head Stand, Sphynx.
Variations.	Forearm Table or Puppy.
	Forearms parallel and/or use wall to learn forearm balance.
	Reclining Down Dog, alternate lifted leg on repetition.

37. **Child's Pose – Balasana** (bala = child)

Chakras/Doshas/Vayus. Root, Sacral, Heart, 3rd Eye/All except Kapha Imbalance/Downward, upward.

Cautions.	Pre-natal, trauma, hip, and knee conditions.
Benefits.	Stretches back, hips, thighs, ankles. Can decrease mental/physical tension.
Cues.	From Table, lean backward onto heels (knees either wide or together).
	Lay torso on or between thighs and rest head.
	Broaden pelvis and lengthen torso, release effort.
Sequence.	Savasana, Hero, Locust.
Variations.	Baby Pose with hands at neck, under face, or arms long next to body.
	Torso and head on bolster, blanket under knees and ankles.
	Bolster or rolled blanket under forehead, hip creases, and ankles.

  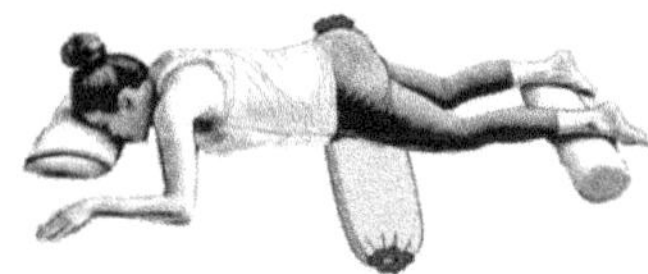

38. Corpse – Savasana (Sava = corpse)

Chakras/Doshas/Vayus. All/All/All.

Cautions.	Pre-natal and back conditions.
Benefits.	Can relieve stress and reduce fatigue and anxiety.
Cues.	Lay down on back, feet open to edges of mat.
	Release arms, rest backs of hands on the floor.
	Soften lower back, lengthen neck, relax torso and legs.
	Soften tongue, nose, ears, forehead, and eyes.
	To come out, roll onto side for a few moments.
	Slowly press up to seated position.
Sequence.	Mantra or meditation.
Variations.	Place bolster under knees to ease lower back tension.
	Elevate torso and/or knees with blocks and bolster.

Relenting Effort

Savasana, or Corpse pose, typically lasts 5 to 10 minutes at the end of class and as a time and space of integration of practice benefits. But laying on your back on a thin mat over hard floor, in stillness, next to strangers, usually in a dimly lit room – can be the most challenging pose of the class. So even though Savasana is at the end, preparation to relent effort begins before class begins and continues throughout the practice. In a "perfect" Savasana, all vayus are present because all internal winds are quiet and balanced.

"Perfecting posture is relaxing,
relenting effort and allowing
attention to merge with the infinite"
- Yoga Sutras 2.46.

Seated and Finishing Series Actions

Pose	Joint Actions				Muscle Actions									
					Upper Front		Upper Back		Lower Front		Lower Back		Side Body	
					Abdominals & fronts of arms, chest, shoulders		Mid/upper back & backs of arms, shoulders		Fronts of pelvis & legs, quads, hip flexors		Backs of legs, glutes, hamstrings		Limbs out from sides (abduction), or to midline (adduction)	
	Spine	Shoulders	Hips	Knees	Contracts	Stretches	Contracts	Stretches	Contracts	Stretches	Contracts	Stretches	Adduction	Abduction
Transition series x7 (no variation)	Flexion	Flexion	Flexion	Flexion	Yes	No	Yes	Yes	Yes	Yes	No	Yes	No	No
Seated Staff	Flexion	Flexion	Flexion	Neutral	No	No	No	No	Yes	No	No	Yes	No	No
Seated Fold A	Flexion	Flexion	Flexion	Neutral	Yes	No	No	Yes	Yes	No	No	Yes	No	No
Seated Fold B	Flexion	Flexion	Flexion	Neutral	Yes	No	No	Yes	Yes	No	No	Yes	No	No
Reverse Plank	Extension	Extension	Extension	Neutral	No	Yes	Yes	No	No	Yes	Yes	No	No	No
Head to Knee A	Flexion	Flexion	Rot/Abd	Flex/Rot	Yes	No	No	Yes	Yes	Yes	Yes	Yes	No	Yes
Sage Twist	Rotation	Abd/Rot	Flex/Add	Flexion	Yes	Yes	Yes	Yes	Yes	Yes	Yes	Yes	Yes	Yes
Boat Pose	Flexion	Flexion	Flexion	Neutral	Yes	No	Yes	No	Yes	No	No	Yes	No	No
Bound Angle	Neutral	Neutral	Rot/Flex	Flex/Rot	Yes	No	No	Yes	Yes	No	No	Yes	No	No
Bridge	Extension	Extension	Extension	Flexion	No	Yes	Yes	No	No	Yes	Yes	No	No	No
Wheel	Extension	Extension	Extension	Flexion	No	Yes	Yes	Yes	No	Yes	Yes	No	No	No
Shoulder Stand	Flexion	Extension	Flexion	Extension	Yes	No	No	No	Yes	No	Yes	No	No	No
Plow	Flexion	Extension	Flexion	Extension	Yes	No	No	Yes	Yes	No	No	Yes	No	No
Fish	Extension	Extension	Neutral	Neutral	No	Yes	Yes	No	Yes	No	No	No	No	No
Dolphin	Flexion	Flexion	Flexion	Extension	Yes	No	Yes	No	Yes	No	No	Yes	No	No
Child's Pose	Extension	Flexion	Flexion	Flex/Rot	Yes	No	No	Yes	Yes	No	No	No	No	No
Corpse pose	Neutral	Rotation	Rotation	Neutral	No	No	No	No	No	No	No	No	No	No
# Flexion	15	14	17	13										
# Extension	5	6	3	3										
# Rotation	1	2	3	3										
# Abduction		1	1											
# Adduction		0	1											
TOTAL # YES					17	4	14	15	19	12	13	16	1	2

Actions do not include those used for structure under typical load or in transition to/from pose.

Primary actions may be multiple (i.e., when legs or arms in differing directions from such as Warrior I).

Practice

1. Breathe

    Review the breathing practices previously covered and take on a breathing research project yourself.

2. Teach

    Review the Seated and Finishing poses. Use caution when practicing and teaching Wheel, Shoulderstand and Plow as these poses are not safe without props and/or variation for many people. First practice variations of Seated and Finishing poses before leading someone else, then teach without demonstration and stop at any pose that is not working to find a variation that provides maximum benefit.

    After class, ask for the following feedback:

    > What was their overall experience of class?
    >
    > What did they like best about your teaching?
    >
    > What is one thing they could tell you to help you grow?

3. Joint Actions
    a) Review the joint actions used in the Seated and Finishing Series, focusing on how major joints action of flexion and extension were equally or not equally utilized.
    b) If you wanted to add a few poses to the Seated and Finishing Series to better equalize flexion and extension of the spine, shoulders, and hips, what might those poses be?

4. Muscle Actions
    a) Review the muscle actions used in the Seated and Finishing Series, focusing on opposing actions. Did any body part receive significantly more contracting than stretching?
    b) If you wanted to add a few poses to your Seated and Finishing Series to better equalize contraction (strengthening) in the upper back body, what might those poses be?

5. Move

    Take a physical yoga class labeled Ashtanga Vinyasa Primary Series. Apply the modifications you have practiced for yourself in any pose that is needed. Before and after class, note sensations in the following areas of your body.

    > Before: My heart feels ____________, my head feels __________, my feet feel ____________.
    >
    > After: My heart feels ____________, my head feels __________, my feet feel ____________.

Chapter 3

Other Poses and Practices

Freedom begins with self if it is to take hold in the world.

The modified Ashtanga Primary Series introduced in Chapter 2 offered 38 poses, any of which can be used in creating your own sequences. But there are many more options for sequences. This chapter invites you into the exploration of pose categories and other practices.

Freedom of Practice

The physical practice of yoga is an exploration that is not confined by any one sequence or style. When you have a variety of practice tools to draw from, your practice can be shaped by what your body and mind need on any given day.

This chapter includes the following Hatha pose categories.

> Backbends (posture, heart expansion)
> Revolved poses (digestion, balance, spinal health)
> Balancing poses (musculoskeletal strength, proprioception, focus)
> Inversions (physical strength/balance, positive energy/self-awareness)

It also offers complimentary schools of physical practice.

> Yin (connective tissue elasticity)
> Kundalini poses and kriyas (specific desired outcomes)
> Nidra (counter stress, reduce anxiety, regulate sleep, etc.)

Related practices for additional options towards harmony and connection are also included.

> Qigong (cultivating vitality through awareness, focus and presence)
> Indigenous practices (symbolism, storytelling, sense of belonging, celebrations)

Important general notes for Other Poses and Practices are:

✓ Other Poses and Practices provided are not meant to be sequenced in order.
✓ Sequence ideas under Other Poses and Practices are a sample of possibilities.
✓ For two-sided poses, directions given are for the right side. Repeat on left side.
✓ Variations shown are intended for similar subtle, energetic, and functional benefits.

Backbends

"Nobody has ever measured, not even poets, how much the heart can hold"
- Zelda Fitzgerald.

Backbends can support ergonomic postural corrections for daily routines while also exposing our heart's natural spaciousness. However, our bodies can hold tightly to tension, so front body expansion is a journey toward the deep meaning of Anahata, the Sanskrit name for the heart chakra (meaning unstruck, unhurt, or unbeaten), and this is why backbends are often called heart-openers. Important notes for backbends are:

- ✓ Safety includes warm up, pauses to allow energy to move, and counterposes for stability.
- ✓ Cautions presented cannot cover all variables and are not a substitute for medical advice.
- ✓ Variations are recommended for pre-natal, osteoporosis and back conditions.
- ✓ If a practitioner is without use of one or more limbs, modify variations to engage available joints.
- ✓ Additional backbend poses (with variations) can be found in the Ashtanga Primary Series poses.

39. Cobra —Bhujangasana (Bhujanga = serpent)

Chakras/Doshas/Vayus. Root, Sacral/All/Inward, downward.

Cautions.	Pre-natal and shoulder conditions.
	When building strength, lower knees first to avoid shoulder injury.
Benefits.	Strengthens upper body, stretches back and adductors.
	Can increase flexibility, ease back pain, and reduce fatigue.
Cues.	From Plank, exhale lower to floor, hands under shoulders.
	Elbow points toward feet, tops of feet on mat.
	Inhale and press into hands, engage core, lift chest.
	Shoulder blades towards ribs, chest open, gaze upward.
	Pelvis, legs, and tops of feet stay grounded on mat.
Sequence.	Downward Dog, Puppy, Dolphin, Child's Pose, and Table.
Variations.	Standing Cobra.
	Cow or Sphynx.
	Chair Cobra with arm variation.
	Bolster under low pelvis or blocks under hands.
	Reclining Cow or Bridge.

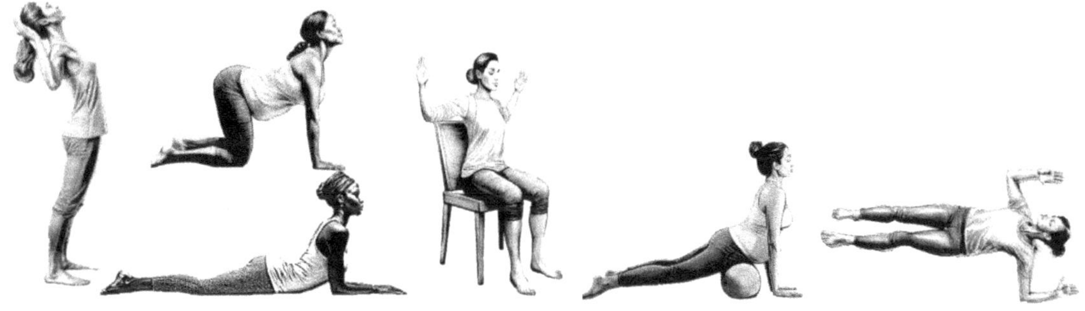

Validating Actions of the Heart

Humans often seek validation in conditioned ways that show up in messaging and actions. Practicing the Yamas of non-harming, truthfulness, non-stealing, moderation, and non-hoarding can powerfully shift one's present moment and future. For example, when teachers cue "Upward Dog or Cobra" during a class, what the teacher likely means to offer is a choice. However, for many practitioners this cueing can instead accomplish indecision, comparison, and internal stories.

While the option for Upward Facing Dog is good, hearing simplicity and feeling a heart opener in Cobra can set the stage for informed choice, safer action, and deeper somatic experience. Cobra is a gentle but powerful way into heart opening that offers real choice – to feel free while also having support. After Cobra is offered, specific cueing for Upward Facing Dog can be offered the next time Cobra comes up in the sequence. After both have been cued individually, one can choose which heart opener feels best. Then, if Cobra or Upward Dog comes up again in the same practice, the only cue needed is "heart-opener" or breath. Though it may feel difficult to trust what was said earlier does not need repeating, silence is when one can be self-taught.

40. Cow – Bitilasana (Bitila = cow)

Chakras/Doshas/Vayus. Sacral, Solar Plexus/All/Inward, downward.

Cautions. Wrist, knee, and back conditions.

Benefits. Can increase spinal flexibility and promote sense of calmness.

Cues. From Table, inhale navel towards floor, neck, and gaze tilt up.

Broaden and lift sit bones, broaden and lower shoulder blades.

Hands actively press downward; elbows have a micro-bend.

Sequence. Cat, Puppy, Balancing Table, or Knees Down Plank.

Variations. Standing Cobra and/or reduce arch.

Chair cobra with arm variation.

Blocks under hands and or forearms.

Reclining Cow or Bridge.

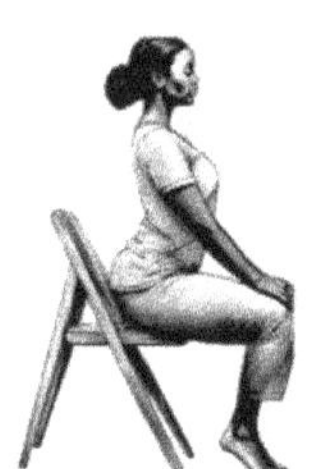

41. Cat - Marjaryasana (Marjari = cat)

Chakras/Doshas/Vayus. Root, 3rd Eye/All/Inward, downward.

Cautions. Wrist, knee, osteoporosis, and back conditions.

Benefits. Can increase spinal flexibility. Can promote sense of calmness.

Cues. From Cow, exhale round spine, neck, and gaze tilt down.

Broaden and lower sit bones, broaden and lift shoulders.

Hands actively press down; elbows have a micro-bend.

Sequence. Rabbit, Cow, Puppy, or Dolphin.

Variations. Standing Cat (hands in front or on thighs), and/or reduce arch.

Chair Cow, hands on thighs, tilt chin down as back rounds.

Blocks under hands and/or blanket under knees.

Reclining knees to chest, or Reclining Cow.

42. Locust - Salabhasana (Salabha = locust)

Chakras/Doshas/Vayus. Solar Plexus/All/Inward, downward, balancing, expanding.

Cautions. Pre-natal, neck or back conditions.

Benefits. Strengthens back body and stimulates abdominal organs.

Cues. On stomach with arms at sides and head down.

Inhale to lift head, chest, hands, and feet.

Reach arms back toward feet, collarbones broaden.

Weight low abdomen and front pelvis, gaze forward.

Sequence. Child's Pose, Downward Dog, Plank, or Puppy.

Variations. Standing backbend with hands on back, Standing Cobra, or extend arms straight forward.

In chair, perform Reverse Plank.

Legs only Locust, hands under hips as props, palms down, and forehead on floor.

Blanket under abdomen for lift, any arm variation.

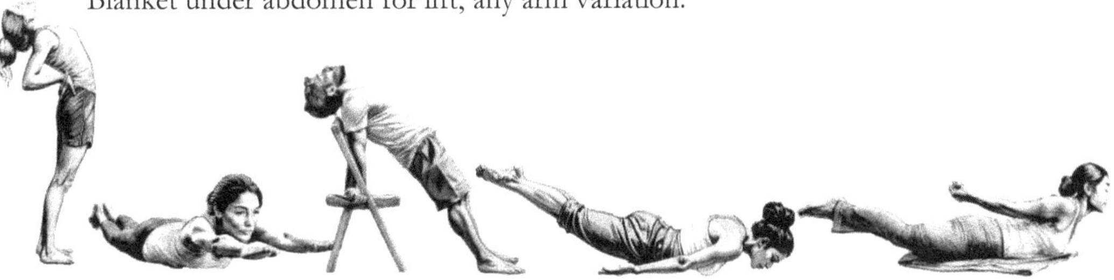

43. Snake - Sarpasana (Sarpa = snake)

Chakras/Doshas/Vayus. Heart/All/ Inward, downward, balancing, and expanding.

Cautions. Pre-natal, back and shoulder conditions.

Benefits. Stretches shoulders, back and chest. Can strengthen thighs and pelvic muscles.

Cues. On stomach with hands clasped behind back and head down.

Inhale to lift chest, broaden pelvis, draw knuckles toward heels.

Engage legs downward, broaden chest, gaze forward.

Sequence. Child's Pose, Downward Dog, Plank, or Puppy.

Variations. Standing Cow or Sphynx Pose.

Chair Cow Pose with hands on chair back.

Blanket under abdomen for lift.

Reclining Fish Pose variation (ankles extended if available) or Cow Pose variations.

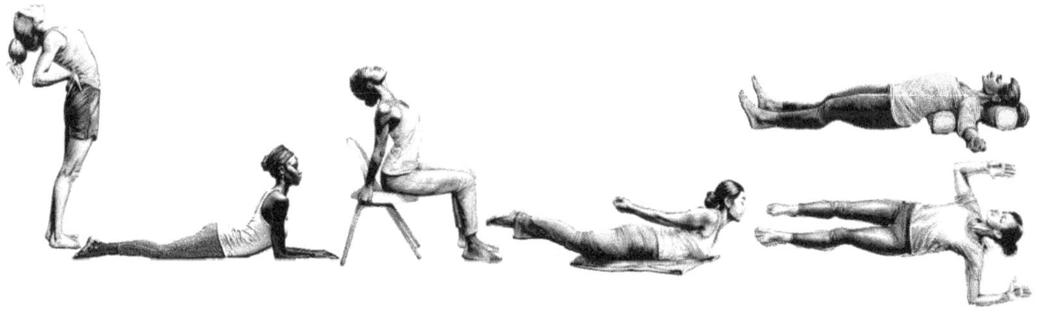

44. Bow - Bharmanasana (Dhanu = bow)

Chakras/Doshas/Vayus. Solar, Heart/All/ Inward, downward, balancing, expanding.

Cautions.   Pre-natal, ankle, shoulder, and heart conditions.

Benefits.   Stretches front body, strengthens back body.

Can improve posture.

Cues.   Lying on stomach, bend knees, reach hands to ankles.

Inhale to lift head, chest, knees, and thighs off the mat.

Lengthen side body, shoulder blades draw in to open chest.

Knees hip width, neck aligns with spine, chin parallel to floor.

Sequence.   Child's Pose, Downward Dog, or Puppy.

Variations.   Dancer or Kneeling Side Bow.

Chair Reverse Plank.

Bolster under pelvis for ease of lift.

Reclining Half Bow or Prone Side Bow.

45. Camel - Ustrasana (Ustra = Camel)

Chakras/Doshas/Vayus. Heart/All/Inward, downward, balancing, upward.

Cautions.   Pre-natal, back and knee conditions.

Benefits.   Can stretch chest/shoulders, improve circulation, decrease stress.

Cues.   From kneeling, rotate thighs inward, press shins and tops of feet down.

Bring hands to lower back (top of pelvis), fingers point to floor.

Lengthen tailbone downward and upper body upward.

Reach hands to heels, chin tucks toward chest.

Thighs are perpendicular to floor; hips are over knees.

Lift up through pelvis, keep lower spine long, neck is neutral.

To come out, bring chin toward chest and take a counter pose.

Sequence.   Child's Pose or Puppy.

Variations.   Hands to lower back (elbows draw inward) and/or raise heels.

Chair Snake.

Hands on yoga blocks outside of feet.

Prone Locust.

46. Wild Thing - Camatkarasana (Camatka = Surprised)

Chakras/Doshas/Vayus. Heart/All/Inward, balancing, expanding.

Cautions. Pre-natal, osteoporosis, back, shoulder or wrist conditions.

Benefits. Strengthens limbs, core. Stretches abdomen, chest, adductors.
Can improve balance and focus.

Cues. From 3-Legged Dog, bend right knee, heel to left glute.
Shift slightly forward over right hand.
Lower right foot until foot is planted on ground.
Left foot presses down, right hand reaches up/toward front.
Shoulder blades draw inward, chest lifts, gaze upwards.
Come out by safely rotating planted arm while chest is lifted.

Sequence. Locust, Gate, 3-Legged Dog, Downward Dog.

Variations. Kneeling Wild Thing (from Side Plank variation).
Sit in chair with left leg straight to left side and right arm reaching slightly behind torso.
Reclining Half Bow or Prone Side Bow.

  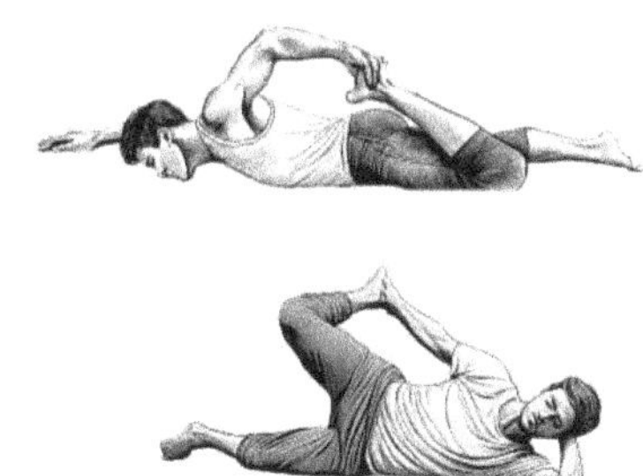

Openness Requires Stability

Backbends are poses that involve spinal extension. The spine is made up of multiple regions, and each region has its own purpose and available degrees of extension. The cervical spine (neck) can extend generously such as in looking up at the sky, and the thoracic spine (mid-back) is designed to extend moderately such as in big stretches after sitting for a long period. The lumbar spine (low-back) is built for stability and so has limited extension ranges, and the sacrum (base of spine within the pelvis) is not supposed to extend at all.

Backbends benefit from small steps that create space in vertebrae first, the use of props for alignment, active muscular engagement, and weaving in of counterposes. Counterposes to backbends are those that allow the spine to rest in neutral (as in lying flat on your stomach or back) or perform flexion (as in supine hugging knees to chest). Countering extension is necessary to neutralize spinal tissues because spinal extension shortens or compresses hip flexors, spinal extensors, and facet joints. Without countering those effects, backbends can create wear and tear on lumbar facet joints and discs and reduce spinal stability over time.

It is also common to experience emotional releases during or after backbends. In the chakra system, the heart acts as an intersection where dense subtle energy - the right to be here, to feel and to act – meets lighter subtle energy - the right to speak, to trust and to be connected. Counterposes weaved amongst backbends can help stabilize emotions and reveal a sanctuary of spacious wholeness that feels unbreakable.

Practice

1. Breathe

Review Cannon Breath, Lion's Breath, and Breath of Joy in Pranayama. Practice each breath for 1-3 minutes (allow time between each for blood pressure to stabilize). Then lead a volunteer through these breaths.

2. Experiment, Create and Teach
    a) Review the new backbends in this section, as well as previous backbends in the Ashtanga Primary Series (Upward Facing Dog, Reverse Plank, Wheel, and Fish). Practice this section's backbends (along with counterposes in between each) and their variations.
    b) Choose 2-3 backbend poses that support a sense of spaciousness in your chest and heart.
    c) Choose 2-3 counter poses to stabilize the spine between backbends (see pose Sequence ideas).
    d) Choose 1-2 breathing techniques that support a sense of positive emotional release for you.
    e) Draft a 15-minute heart opening sequence that includes backbends, counterposes and complimentary breathing techniques in a fluid sequence that offers unhurried/equal time for each.
    f) Review your sequence for equanimity in joints and muscles, and for the health condition you are most interested in to adjust your sequence accordingly.
    g) Lead someone else through your heart-opening sequence with minimal demonstration and without notes. If your volunteer cannot do all poses and transitions with ease, offer pose variations.
    h) Ask your volunteer for feedback in the following areas:
        What was their overall experience of class?
        What did they like best about your teaching?
        What is one thing they could tell you to help you grow?
3. Move

Take a class labeled as a Heart Opener. Before and after class, note sensations in your body.

Before: My heart feels ___________, my head feels __________, my feet feel ____________.

After: My heart feels ___________, my head feels __________, my feet feel ___________.

Balancing Poses

Staying high is a practice of both will and surrender - equally.

Balancing poses can improve spinal and core stability, circulation, bone health, stamina, proprioception, coordination, and focus. They can also offer a sense of liberation and fortitude as if you could fly like an eagle. But to stay high and suspended in space, one must surrender mental gravity (negativity, judgements, comparisons, self-shaming, distractions, etc.). One way to hack mental gravity is to expose natural elevating capabilities through small steps that lead to the embodiment of balance within.

Regardless of physical characteristics, all bodies can achieve physical balance through internal adjustments of energy and surrendering holds on mental gravity. Important notes for balancing poses are:

- ✓ Balances are often best approached through the progression of small steps, beginning with variations closer to or on the ground, where the brain can get on-board before suspending body parts in the air.
- ✓ Cautions presented cannot cover all variables and are not a substitute for medical advice.
- ✓ Variations are recommended for brain and joint conditions.
- ✓ If a practitioner is without use of one or more limbs, modify variations to engage available joints.
- ✓ Additional balancing poses (with variations) can be found in the Ashtanga Primary Series poses.

47. Easy Pose - Sukhasana (Sukha = easy)

Chakras/Doshas/Vayus. All/All/Downward, balancing.

Cautions.	Knee, hip, ankle, and lower back conditions.
Benefits.	Can decrease tension and improve posture, flexibility, and focus.
Cues.	Legs cross, sit bones firmly grounded.
	Hands rest on thighs, shoulders relax.
	Lengthen spine from tailbone to top of head.
	Gaze forward, jaw is relaxed, tongue rests.
Sequence.	Butterfly, Seated Twist, Dandasana, Meditation, Pranayama.
Variations.	Any mudra and/or wall behind back with blanket under tailbone.
	In chair, either with feet on floor or crossed in seat.
	Blocks under knees and/or sitting on bolster with knees lower.
	Recline with head elevated (use bolsters, blocks, and blankets).

48. Hero – Virasana (Vira = hero or warrior)

Chakras/Doshas/Vayus. All/All except if Vata Imbalance/Downward, balancing.

Cautions.	Knee, ankle, hip, or lower back conditions.
Benefits.	Stretches fronts of legs and ankles; promotes calm focus.
Cues.	From Table, widen feet a few inches, lean sit bones backward.
	Draw navel toward spine, lengthen spine from tailbone to crown.
	Shoulders and jaw relaxes, hands rest on thighs, gaze forward.
Sequence.	Reclining Hero, Camel, Cobra, Sat Kriya, Meditation.
Variations.	Hands in any mudra and kneeling or sitting on heels.
	Mountain pose in chair.
	Blanket under knees and/or sit on block for support.
	Reclining hero with or without bolster under torso and head.

  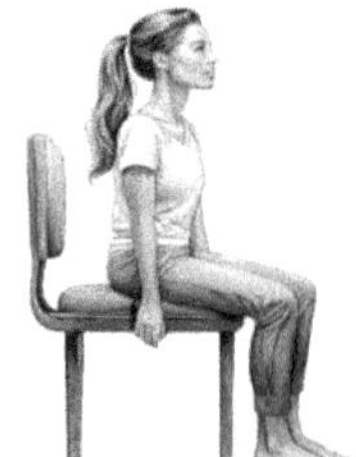  

49. Table - Bharmanasana (Bharman = table)

Chakras/Doshas/Vayus. Root/All/Downward, balancing.

Cautions. Knee and wrist conditions.

Benefits. Can strengthen core and improve spinal tension.

Cues. From Downward Dog, lower knees to ground.

Place tops of feet on floor, knees align under hips.

Shoulders align over hands, fingers are wide.

Back and head are neutral; gaze is toward floor.

Sequence. Cat/Cow, Balancing Table, Tiger, Gate, Frog or Hero.

Variations. Chair variation (90-degree flexion of hips, arms perpendicular in front with wrists flexed).

In chair, sit bones on edge, lift arms perpendicular to floor, wrists flex, palms face front.

Blanket under knees and blanket, blocks or rolled mat under wrists for joint support.

Reclining Table/Plank, lower leg(s) are perpendicular to floor, arms are straight up.

Turn the Tables

Psoas muscles are hip flexors that stabilize our bodies by connecting our torso to our legs through our pelvis. They can become chronically tense from physical injury, an overstimulated sympathetic nervous system or trauma. Further contracting the psoas through loaded flexion can exasperate physical instability and pain.

In Table or Downward Facing Dog, knee to nose or knee to elbow movements may aggravate pre-existing low back, sacroiliac instability, and/or hip flexor conditions as they engage the hip flexors, spine, and abdominals in loaded flexion. However, when you turn the table upside down, often called the Dead Bug position, muscle contractions are not dependent upon lumbar spine loading, making upside down variations a great option for those with lower back or psoas conditions. Most poses can be turned upside down or on their sides for similar or improved benefits. You can also change the position of limbs, including lifting knees for hovering Table.

While most yoga poses offer multiple variations to maximum value of those poses, Balancing Table seems to offer some of the most flexibility in variations to meet the basic pose's aims of improving balance and focus while strengthening the limbs and core. For example, using opposing muscles for the Tiger variation for above torso movement strengthens both the front and back torso, as well as reduces psoas tension.

50. Balancing Table - **Dandayamana Bharmanasana** (Danda = stick, yamana = balancing, bharma = table)

Chakras/Doshas/Vayus. Root, Solar/All/Downward, balancing, expanding.

Cautions.	Knee, shoulder, and wrist conditions.
Benefits.	Can improve balance/focus and strengthen limbs /core.
Cues.	From Table, extend right leg back, buttocks even.
	Left arm and right leg extends straight.
	Draw navel toward spine, engage entire body.
	Gaze slightly forward with neutral neck.
Sequence.	Tiger, Plank, Gate, Side Plank.
Variations.	Calf stretch, right toes down, heel presses back.
	Hand to foot in Tiger pose or Balancing Plank.
	Tiger variation (lifted elbow/lifted knee bent, lifted hand/foot up, stabilize with glutes).
	In chair, raise left arm and right leg perpendicular to floor (flex toes).
	Blanket under knees and blocks or rolled mat under wrists for support.
	Recline with right leg extended on mat, flex feet, extend left arm overhead.

\

51. Gate - Dandayamana Bharmanasana (Danda = stick, yamana = balancing, bharma = table)

Chakras/Doshas/Vayus. Root, Solar, Heart, Throat/All/Balancing, downward, expanding.

Cautions.	Knee or shoulder conditions.
Benefits.	Stretches side body. Can improve focus, coordination, and strength.
Cues.	From Table, rotate left foot to outside of mat for "kickstand."
	Extend right leg straight behind left knee, rotate foot, ground sole.
	Lift right arm upward (and/or forward over right ear).
	Entire body is in one line, gaze and chin are upward.
Sequence.	Side Plank, Half Frog, Table, Revolved Low Lunge.
Variations.	Half Frog/Side Gate (leg extension only).
	Open Gate, lift torso, raise left arm for side bend.
	Chair Extended Side Angle.
	Blanket under knee and block under wrist.
	Reclining Half Moon.

52. Side Plank - Vasistha (Most excellent)

Chakras/Doshas/Vayus. Solar Plexus, Throat/All/Balancing, downward, expanding.

Cautions.	Shoulder, wrist, knee, and ankle conditions.
Benefits.	Can strengthen entire body and improve balance.
Cues.	From Plank, exhale to rotate left foot to outside edge.
	Right foot stacks on top of left, torso follows to right side.
	Engage strongly from thighs through heels.
	Left knuckles/index finger press down, shoulder girdle is firm.
	Top hand reaches up through fingers, neck/gaze turn upward.
Sequence.	Leg lifted Side Plank, Plank, Side Gate.
Variations.	Top arm reaches forward over ear and/or lift top leg.
	Side Gate/Plank with knee down.
	Chair Extended Side Angle.
	Forearm Plank, option to lift top leg.
	Reclining Side Plank with bottom arm in any variation.

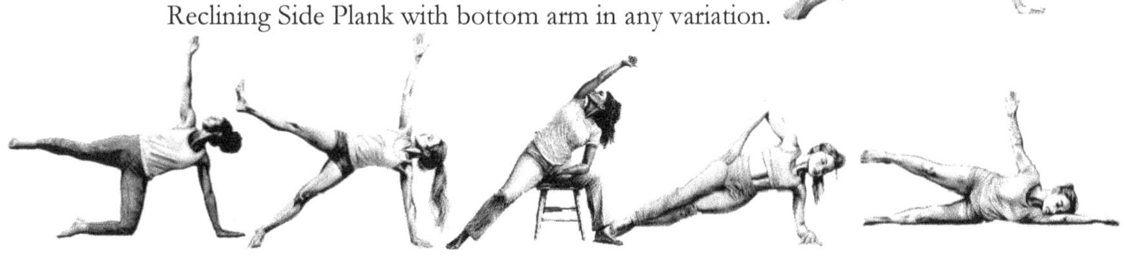

53. 3-Legged Dog - Tri Pada Adho Mukha Svanasana (3 Legged Downward Dog Facing)

Chakras/Doshas/Vayus. Root, Solar, Heart, Throat/All/Downward, upward, balancing, expanding.

Cautions. Pre-natal, shoulder and wrist conditions.

Benefits. Can strengthen entire body and improve stamina, energy, and balance.

Cues. From Downward Dog, inhale to extend right leg up, right foot flexed.

Fingers wide, index fingers forward, finger pads press down.

Broaden shoulder blades; torso, arms and legs are engaged.

Neck is neutral, gaze toward knees.

Sequence. Wild Thing, Low Lunge, Runner's Lunge, Squat.

Variations. Balancing Table or Balancing Puppy.

Bend knee and lower heel toward other buttock.

Chair Downward Facing Dog.

Blocks under wrists or forearms for support.

Recline on stomach, one right leg upwards.

54. Low Lunge - Variation of Anjaneyasana (Anjaneya = praise)

Chakras/Doshas/Vayus. Root, Solar Plexus/All/Balancing, downward, expanding.

Cautions. Knee and shoulder conditions.

Benefits. Stretches and strengthens legs and core; can increase calm and focus.

Cues. From Table, place right foot inside right hand.

Inhale arms up, palms face, fingers are upward and active.

Right knee aligns over heel, gaze forward or to fingertips.

Sequence. Half Splits, Table, Lizard, Runner's Lunge, Balancing Table or Gate.

Variations. Psoas side stretch (left hand high, lean forward and towards right side).

Reach left hand back to left foot or keep hands on thigh..

Chair Lunge.

Hands on top thigh and blanket under knee.

Reclining Chair or Bow (either stretch or strengthen emphasis).

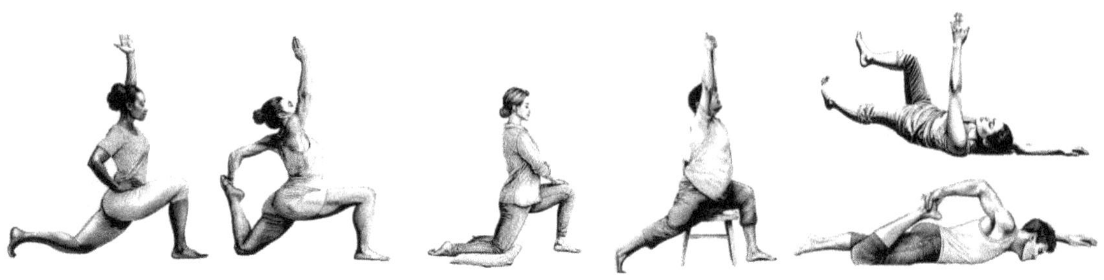

55. Half Splits - Ardha Hanumanasana (Half Monkey God Pose)

Chakras/Doshas/Vayus. Root, Sacral/All except Vata Imbalance/Balancing, downward, expanding.

Cautions. Pre-natal, sacroiliac and knee conditions.

Benefits. Can stretch glutes, hamstrings, and calves.

Can increase balance and decrease tension.

Cues. From Low Lunge, place hands to frame front foot.

Flex right foot, lean back to straighten left leg.

Left leg straightens, left foot is flexed.

Inhale lengthen spine, exhale hinge at waist, chest lowers.

Shoulders and hips align, gaze forward.

Sequence. Cobra, Lizard, Gate, Table, or 3-Legged Down Dog.

Variations. Standing Splits.

Chair Hand to Knee Pose.

Blocks under hands and/or blanket under knee for support.

Reclined Hand to Big Toe.

56. Lizard - Utthan Pristhasana (Utthan = stretch out, Pristha = page of the book or back body)

Chakras/Doshas/Vayus. Root, Sacral/All except Vata Imbalance/Downward, balancing, expanding.

Cautions. Pre-natal, hip, lower back, and knee conditions.

Benefits. Can stretch hips and legs and decrease tension and stimulate digestion.

Cues. From Low Lunge, heel toe right foot near long edge of mat.

Place right hand inside right foot, lower to forearms.

Right inner calf hugs right arm.

Chest is open, gaze is neutral.

Sequence. Sphynx, Half Splits, Table, Twisted Dragon.

Variations. Keep arms straight and/or knee down.

Chair Lunge.

Block under hands or forearms.

Recline in Half Happy Baby (strap or hands to foot).

57. Runner's Lunge - Variation of Arda Mandalasana (Arda = Half, Mandala = Circle)

Chakras/Doshas/Vayus. Root, Sacral/All/Balancing, downward, expanding.

Cautions.	Pre-natal, knee, shoulder, hip, and low back conditions.
Benefits.	Can increase stamina, limb, and core strength.
Cues.	From Half Lift, plant hands to frame front foot.
	Extend left leg straight back, back heel over back toes.
	Engage quads upward, draw navel toward spine.
	Left hip draws forward; right hip draws back.
	Extend tailbone to crown, gaze forward.
Sequence.	Revolved lunge, Lizard, High Lunge, 3-Legged Plank.
Variations.	Low lunge with hands on top thigh.
	Chair Lunge.
	Blocks under hands to elevate torso.
	Recline in Half Happy Baby (strap or hands to foot if needed).

58. Warrior III - Virabhadrasana III (Virabhadra = mythical Vedic deity)

Chakras/Doshas/Vayus. Root, Solar /All/Balancing, expanding.

Cautions.	Knee, ankle, hip, or shoulder conditions.
Benefits.	Can strengthen arms, core and legs, and improve balance, focus, and posture.
Cues.	From Mountain, weight right foot (micro-bend knee).
	Extend left leg back as torso hinges forward.
	Whole body except standing leg is parallel to floor.
	Lifted foot flexes, heel presses back, standing leg engages/lifts.
	Active arms reach forward, neck is neutral, gaze at floor.
Sequence.	Forward Bend, High lunge, Standing Splits, Balancing Half Moon.
Variations.	Prayer hands or airplane arms.
	Half Pyramid (offers leg stretch but not leg strengthening).
	Hands on block or foot on wall for stability.
	Recline in 3-Legged Dog variation.

59. Crescent Lunge - Anjaneyasana (Anjaneya = praise)

    Chakras/Doshas/Vayus. Root, Sacral, Solar /All/Downward, balancing, expanding.

Cautions.	Knee, ankle, shoulder, hip, and low back conditions.
Benefits.	Can strengthen torso and limbs, stretch adductors, increase energy.
Cues.	From Runner's Lunge, inhale torso and arms upward.
	Palms face with active fingers, extend spine up through top of head.
	Neutral tailbone, navel toward spine, shoulder blades travel down.
	Gaze ahead or upward at fingertips.
Sequence.	Runner's Lunge, Plank, Revolved Lunge, 3-Legged Dog.
Variations.	Cactus or airplane arms and/or Low Lunge.
	Chair Lunge.
	Blocks or weights in each hand for core strengthening.
	Recline in Half Bow.

60. Humble Warrior - Baddha Virabhadrasana (Bound Warrior)

    Chakras/Doshas/Vayus. Root, Sacral, Heart/All/Downward, balancing, upward.

Cautions.	Pre-natal, back, hip, knee, and shoulder conditions.
Benefits.	Can strengthen legs and core and stretch legs, chest, and arms.
	Can improve balance and focus.
Cues.	From Warrior I, exhale hands behind back in a bind.
	Inhale to lengthen spine, exhale to hinge forward.
	Engage entire body, back heel weights and equalizes weight.
	Knuckles reach toward heels, gaze down to mat.
Sequence.	Lizard, Dragon, Squat, Forward Bend, Plank, Table.
Variations.	Airplane arms or grasping opposite forearms behind back.
	Low Lunge with above basics.
	Chair Lunge, bring arms behind in any option and hinge at hips.
	Reclining Half or full Happy Baby.

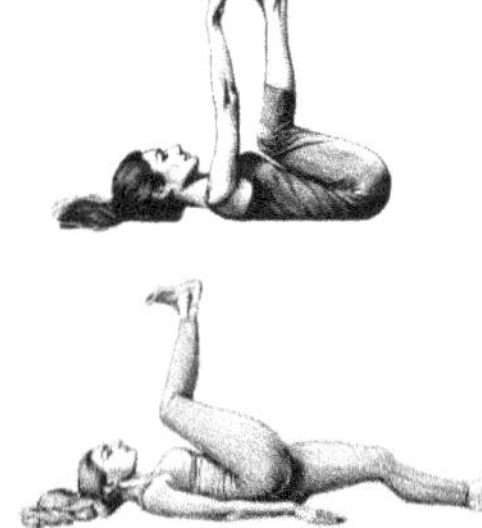

61. Standing Splits -**Urdhva Prasarita Eka Padasana** (Urdhva=up, Prasarita=expanded, Eka=one, Pada=foot/leg)

Chakras/Doshas/Vayus. Root, 3rd Eye/All except Vata or Pitta Imbalance/Downward, upward, balancing.

Cautions.	Pre-natal, back, hip, knee, heart, and eye conditions.
Benefits.	Can strengthen legs, reduce tension, and improve concentration.
Cues.	From Forward Bend, place fingers in front of feet, weight right foot.
	Inhale to raise left leg behind and upward into a split.
	Internally rotate left thigh, equalize leg energy for squared hips.
	Wrap hands behind standing leg, gaze at calf.
Sequence.	Forward Bend, Runner's Lunge, Balancing Half Moon.
Variations.	Lessen angle of fold or do Half Splits.
	Chair Hand to Knee pose.
	Blocks under hands for stability.
	Reclined Hand to Big Toe.

62. Eagle - Garudasana (Garuda = the mythic King of the Birds)

Chakras/Doshas/Vayus. Root, Sacral, 3rd Eye/All except if Vata Imbalance/Balancing.

Cautions.	Pre-natal, back, hip, knee, and shoulder conditions.
Benefits.	Stretches thighs, hips, shoulders/upper back. Can improve focus, balance.
Cues.	Cross arms in front, right under left, bend elbows and press palms together.
	Bend knees, cross right leg over left to wrap right foot behind left.
	Press down through left leg, square hips, and chest.
	Shoulder blades down and back, navel toward spine.
	Elbows outward and fingers upward.
Sequence.	Warrior III, High Lunge, or Mountain.
Variations.	Arns variations (self-hug, prayer, or hands wrapped) and/or Chair 90/90.
	Chair pose with right foot on left thigh and any arm variation.
	In chair, any arm or leg variation.
	Foot on block for balance.
	Recline on back, any arm or leg variation.

 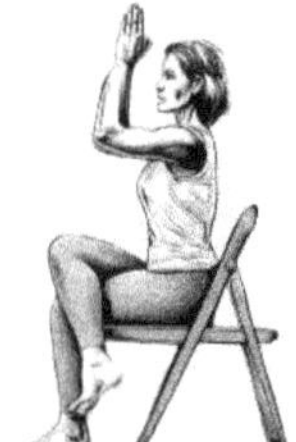  

63. Dancer - Natarajasana (Nata=dancer, Raja=king)

Chakras/Doshas/Vayus. Sacral, Solar Plexus, Heart/All/Inward, balancing, expanding.

Cautions. Back, hip, knee, and shoulder conditions.

Benefits. Can stretch and strengthen limbs and increase coordination.

Cues. From Mountain, weight right foot, bend left knee.

Bring left heel toward buttock, left hand to left ankle.

Lift right arm overhead, point fingers upward, palm faces left.

Left foot up presses up/away as torso leans forward, chest faces front.

Maintain inward and downward stability, gaze at a point ahead.

Sequence. Tree, Warrior III, Mountain, High Lunge.

Variations. Low Lunge variation or bring hands upward and back to grasp right foot.

Chair Lunge, rotate left shoulder, extend arm back (or strap to left foot).

Bolster under hips for prone Dancer; OR hand on wall for balance.

Recline in Half Bow.

64. Bird of Paradise – Svarga Dvijasana (Svarga = Heaven , Dvija = Twice Born)

Chakras/Doshas/Vayus. Sacral, Solar /All except Vata Imbalance/Balancing, expanding.

Cautions. Pre-natal, knee, hip, and lower back conditions.

Benefits. Strengthens legs and core, stretches groin, can improve balance.

Cues. Begin in Extended Side Angle on right.

Bend right elbow to bring right hand under thigh, fingers point up.

Bend left elbow to bring left hand behind back to grasp right hand.

Place weight on left leg, step right leg toward left.

Balance on left foot, elevate torso and right leg.

Straighten right leg, foot is flexed, gaze forward.

Sequence. Forward Bend, Standing Seal, Goddess, or Tree.

Variations. Hand to right knee, knee stays bent.

Chair Hasta B with strap.

Reclined Hand to Big Toe, open right leg to right side.

65. Tree - Vrksasana (Vrksa = tree)

Chakras/Doshas/Vayus. Sacral, Solar Plexus/All/Downward, balancing.

Cautions. Knee and ankle conditions.

Benefits. Can improve leg strength, posture, mood, and balance.

Cues. From Mountain, place weight on left foot, micro bend in left knee.

Bend right knee to place right foot on right inner thigh.

Hip points and left toes face forward, left foot hugs inner thigh.

Palms face at heart center, gaze is forward.

Sequence. Goddess, Dancer, Cresent Lunge, Eagle.

Variations. Open arms (like branches) and/or lifted foot lower on leg.

In chair, cross right ankle over left thigh.

Place block under foot for support or use a wall for balance.

Recline in Fallen Tree.

66. Balancing Half Moon - Ardha Chandrasana (Ard ha=half, Chandra = moon)

Chakras/Doshas/Vayus. Solar Plexus, Heart/All/ Balancing, downward, upward, expanding.

Cautions. Knee, hip, and neck conditions.

Benefits. Can reduce tension and fatigue and improve coordination.

Cues. From Halfway Lift, place hands under nose.

Micro-bend right knee, press into right foot/right hand.

Lift left leg parallel to floor, left heel active/flexed.

Lift left hand palm upward to open torso, stack hips.

Shoulder blades firmly into back, gaze turns upward.

Sequence. Warrior II, Reverse Warrior, Forward Bend.

Variations. Side Plank variation.

Bend left knee, bring top hand to top foot for stretch.

Place hand on block next to wall for balance.

Recline in Hasta B.

67. **Reverse Warrior - Viparita Virabhadrasana** (Viparita = reverse)

Chakras/Doshas/Vayus. Solar Plexus, Heart/All/ Inward, downward, balancing, expanding.

Cautions. Shoulder and lower back conditions.

Benefits. Stretches legs, shoulders/chest; can increase circulation and perseverance.

Cues. From Warrior II, inhale right hand up to lengthen side of torso.

Left arm reaches actively down back leg toward floor.

Soften shoulders down back, gaze at lifted fingertips.

Sequence. Warrior II, Runner's Lunge, Plank, 3-Legged Downward Dog.

Variations. Lessen bend in front knee or straighten front leg.

One hand behind back in a bind.

In chair Warrior II, extend right hand up, left-hand down.

Reclining Palm Tree Stretch (bend right knee if desired).

68. **Squat - Malasana** (Malasana = Garland)

Chakras/Doshas/Vayus. Root, Sacral/All/Downward, balancing.

Cautions. Low back and knee conditions.

Benefits. Can tone and strengthen lower body; increase pelvic circulation and focus.

Cues. From Mountain, heel toe feet to wider than hip-width.

Turn toes out slightly, press palms together.

Exhale and lower hips, elbows inside knees.

Lengthen spine, relax shoulders, draw navel in.

Expand chest, shift weight to heels.

Sequence. Crow, Easy Pose, Plank, Frog, Tabletop.

Variations. Variation of Goddess or Horse.

On edge of chair seat, widen space between knees and feet.

Place block under sacrum for support.

Recline in Happy Baby.

69. Goddess or Horse - Utkata Konasana (Utkata - powerful or fierce, Kona - angle)

Chakras/Doshas/Vayus. Sacral, Solar /All/ Downward, balancing.

Cautions.	Hip and knee conditions.
Benefits.	Strengthens legs and core; can increase circulation and focus.
Cues.	From Star, exhale bend knees until thighs parallel to floor.
	Bend elbows, extend arms to sides at shoulder-height.
	Palms face out, fingers toward ceiling or Gyan mudra.
	Neutralize pelvis, press hips forward, draw thighs backward.
Sequence.	Wide-legged Forward Fold, 5-Pointed Star, Qi Laughter.
Variations.	Lessen degree of knee and elbow bend.
	On edge of chair seat, widen space between knees and feet.
	Hands in prayer and/or standing on tip toes.
	Recline in Bound Angle.

70. Palm Tree and Palm Side Bend - Parsva Talasana (Parsva = Side, Tala = Palm)

Chakras/Doshas/Vayus. Root, Solar /All/Balancing, expanding.

Cautions.	Shoulder conditions.
Benefits.	Full body stretch to improve coordination, spine flexibility.
Cues.	From Tall Mountain, interlace fingers, turn palms upward.
	Exhale, lean arms and torso to right, weight both feet.
	Inhale center (option to raise heels), exhale hands/torso to left.
Sequence.	Tree, Chair, Warrior III, Eagle, Radiance Charger.
Variations.	Raise arm on stretched side only.
	In chair, arms upward, maintain downward pressure in sit bones.
	Strap between hands for shoulder support.
	Reclining Tall Mountain, stabilize hips, scoot hands/feet to right.

71. Happy Baby - Bharmanasana (Danda = stick, yamana = balancing, bharma = table)
Chakras/Doshas/Vayus. Root, Sacral/All/Downward, upward.

Cautions.	Knee, ankle, or shoulder conditions.
Benefits.	Stretches arms, lower back, and glutes.
	Can decrease tension and promote a sense of ease and joy.
Cues.	From laying on back, bend knees into chest.
	Grasp big toes with index finger and thumb.
	Gently pull feet and knees wide, soles of feet upwards.
	Back and back of head grounded, gaze upward.
	Gently rock from side to side like a baby playing.
Sequence.	Bridge, Spinal Twist, Savasana.
Variations.	Hands below thighs or on knees, or outside of feet.

72. Reclining Pigeon - Supta Kapotasana (Supta = reclined, Kapota = pigeon)

Chakras/Doshas/Vayus. Root, Sacral/All/Downward, balancing.

Cautions.	Prenatal and knee conditions.
Benefits.	Stretches hips, glutes, IT band, hamstrings, and low back.
	Can reduce stress and increase circulation.
Cues.	From laying on back, bend knees, heels close to buttocks.
	Place right foot onto left thigh, flex right foot.
	Reach hands behind left thigh to lift left leg.
	Head and shoulders remain on floor.
	Back stays flat or neutral, head and neck align with spine.
Sequence.	Bridge, Supine Twist, Legs Up the Wall, Reclining Palm Tree, Reclining Tree.
Variations.	Left foot and hands remain on floor alongside body.
	In chair, perform pose and lean forward to bolster to deepen stretch.
	Reclining with less bend in upward knee.

Resting Birds

"Regular" Pigeon pose is not described in this book due to high injury risk for joint structures. If you are familiar with prop placement in this pose and the health of your joint ligaments and tendons, there are reasonably safe ways to perform the standard Pigeon pose. However, Reclining Pigeon provides less weighted rotation of knees and hips and is often more beneficial for mind and body, especially for Vatas and Pittas. If interested in Ayurvedic wisdom, you might enjoy this book's companion, *The Guru is You: Yoga for Self-Discovery and Purposeful Living.*

Practice

1. Gaze

Review Drishtis in Subtle Energy. Practice 3 different drishtis for 1 minute each.

2. Experiment, Create and Teach

a) Review the new balances in this section, as well as previous balances in the Ashtanga Primary Series (most are in the Standing Series). Practice this section's balances and their variations.

b) Choose 2-3 balancing poses that support musculoskeletal strength and stamina, proprioception and focus, and a sense of embodied exaltation.

c) Choose 2-3 transition poses to create a fluid sequence (see each pose's Sequence ideas).

d) Choose 1-2 drishtis that support a sense of effortless laser-pointed awareness and balance for you.

e) Draft a 15-minute balancing sequence that includes balancing poses, transitions and complimentary drishti techniques in a fluid sequence that offers unhurried/equal time for each.

f) Review your sequence for equanimity in joints and muscles, and for the health condition you are most interested in to adjust your sequence accordingly.

g) Lead someone else through your balancing sequence with minimal demonstration and without notes. If your volunteer cannot do all poses and transitions with ease, offer pose variations.

h) Ask your volunteer for feedback in the following areas:

What was their overall experience of class?

What did they like best about your teaching?

What is one thing they could tell you to help you grow?

3. Move

Take a class labeled Balances. Before and after class, note sensations in your body.

Before: My heart feels ___________, my head feels _________, my feet feel ___________.

After: My heart feels __________, my head feels _________, my feet feel __________.

Revolved Poses

We keep trying to get what we need from out there. It's not possible.
The way to wholeness is in here.

The act of steering oneself inward in revolved poses (also called twists) can support digestion, balance, and spinal health, and promote a sense of internal alignment and prosperity. However, what your back should look like in a twist cannot be found by looking at anyone else. Spinal structures are typically not visible without special imaging that can show impacts of lifestyle patterns, injuries, and health conditions on your spinal structures. So oversteering or forcing parts of your spine into a twist too far or too soon may be counter to benefits and harmony. However, even without viewing images of your spine, when you are in a twist in a way that is best for your spine, often a sense of inner peace can radiate outwardly. To progress into your own revolution, try using the following formula.

+ Stabilize the spine by aligning shoulders over pelvis.

+ Lengthen the spine on inhale to maximize space between vertebrae.

+ Twist on an exhale from the level of the navel and up.

+ <u>Finish into the twist as gaze follows.</u>

= Revolved Pose spinal alignment

Other important notes for revolved poses are:

✓ Start with progressive variations to learn alignment before adding deeper twists into a practice..

✓ Some practitioners are uncertain as how to twist from the navel area, so after stabilizing and lengthening, try hinging forward about 45 degrees before twisting to more naturally engages the thoracic spine.

✓ To come out of a twist, return to center on an inhale for core stability that supports the spine.

✓ Cautions presented cannot cover all variables and are not a substitute for medical advice.

✓ Variations recommended for abdominal, back, and pelvic conditions and for prenatal and osteoporosis.

✓ If a practitioner is without use of one or more limbs, modify variations to engage available joints.

✓ Additional revolved poses (with variations) can be found in the Ashtanga Primary Series poses.

✓ Some revolved poses are not provided in this book on purpose due to injury risks.

73. Revolved Lunge – Parivrtta Utthita Sanchalanasana (Parivrtta=revolved, Utthita=raised, Sanchalan=horse riding)

Chakras/Doshas/Vayus. Solar Plexus, Heart/All except Vata Imbalance/Balancing, downward.

Cautions. Knee, back, hip or shoulder conditions.

Benefits. Can strengthen arms, legs, and core; can improve focus and coordination.

Cues. From Crescent Lunge on right, inhale to lengthen spine.

Place right hand on hip, extend left arm in front of torso.

Exhale to hinge forward with neutral spine to 45 degrees.

Rotate right shoulder up and left shoulder down (stack shoulders).

Left hand is outside of right calf, right hand reaches upward.

Legs are engaged and stable, neck and gaze turn upward.

Sequence. Runner's Lunge, Plank, Balancing Table, or Down Dog.

Variations. Stay high to limit twist or standing Revolved Hasta.

Lower back knee, top hand on hip or in prayer.

In chair, bend right knee, place left elbow on right knee.

Block under hand for lift.

Reclining Twist.

74. Revolved Balancing Half Moon - **Parivrtta Ardha Chandrasana** (Parivrtta=Revolved, Ardha=Half, Chandra=Moon)

Chakras/Doshas/Vayus. Solar, Heart/All except Vata Imbalance/Balancing, downward, expanding.

Cautions. Pre-natal, knee, ankle, shoulder, or back conditions.

Benefits. Can strengthen legs, relieve spinal tension, improve coordination and digestion.

Cues. From Half Lift, place left hand on floor, right hand on right hip.
Weight right leg (micro bend knee), raise left leg with knee straight.
Inhale to lengthen spine, exhale right elbow up as torso rotates left.
Reach right arm up, gaze at right hand.

Sequence. Runner's Lunge, Plank, 5-Pointed Star.

Variations. Stay in prep position with raised hand on hip; or Hasta Twist.
Chair Hand to Big Toe variation.
Block under hand and/or stand with right side to wall.
Recline in Hand to Big Toe variation.

75. Seated Twist - **Parivrtta Sukhasana** (Parivrtta = revolved, Sukha = easy)

Chakras/Doshas/Vayus. Root, Solar /All/Downward.

Cautions. Pre-natal, knee, ankle, hip, or back conditions.

Benefits. Can increase spine flexibility.

Cues. From Easy Pose, inhale arms up, spine lengthens, shoulders relaxed.
Exhale torso right, left hand lowers to knee, right hand to floor.
Sit bones, shoulders and hips are even, gaze right.

Sequence. Meditation, Butterfly, Deer, Cowface.

Variations. Stretch out legs and/or raise tailbone on blanket.
Chair Spinal Twist.
Hands on shoulders, elbows point outward, prior to twist.
Recline in Supine Twist.

76. Supine Twist - Supta Matsyendrasana (an ancient yoga master – Matseyendra)

Chakras/Doshas/Vayus. Root/All/Downward, balancing.

Cautions.	Pre-natal, lower back and hip conditions
Benefits.	Stretches back, hips and upper leg muscles. Can decrease tension.
Cues.	Lay on right side of body, right side of head rests on floor.
	Arms extend straight forward at shoulders, left arm on top of right arm.
	Hips flex, bent knees in line with hips, left leg on top of right leg.
	Feet align under knees.
	Open left arm to left side floor.
	Head and gaze left turn left.
	Place right hand on left knee.
Sequence.	Bridge, Reclining Tree, Reclining Palm Tree, Savasana.
Variations.	Knees bent with feet wide, lower knees to one side, gaze in other direction.
	Chair Spinal Twist.
	Perform with left leg long and place bolster or blocks under knee for support.

Back It Up

There are many ways to get into a Supine Twist and the cues offered here are intended to support spinal stability for most bodies. This book does <u>not</u> recommend lifting feet or crossing legs before rotating the spine when laying on the back. Although these variations are commonly cued, lifting feet off the mat and/or crossing legs before supine twisting can increase torque through sacroiliac joints and the lower lumbar spine, which may contribute to SI and low back instability.

Our pelvic and lumbar stability is key to daily life functions, so little things like lifting your feet before a twist can add up over time and decrease physical resilience. Keeping at least one foot grounded (or both feet when possible) provides a stable base from which the spine can rotate, which allows the spinal revolution to be distributed more evenly.

Practice

1. Energy Circuits

   Review Gyan and Shuni mudras. Practice each for 1-3 minutes.

2. Experiment, Create and Teach
   a) Review the new revolved poses in this section, as well as previous revolved poses in the Ashtanga Primary Series (in both the Standing and Seated Series). Practice this section's revolved poses (along with transitions that include focused spinal stability in between each) and their variations.
   b) Choose 2-3 revolved poses that support a sense of courageous and unique inward revolution.
   c) Choose 2-3 transitions to stabilize the spine between revolved poses (see pose Sequence ideas).
   d) Choose 1-2 mudras that support a sense of patience, intuition, and inward focus for you.
   e) Draft a 15-minute Twist sequence that includes revolved poses, transitions and a complimentary mudra in a fluid sequence that offers unhurried and equal time for each.
   f) Review your sequence for equanimity in joints and muscles, and for the health condition you are most interested in to adjust your sequence accordingly.
   g) Lead someone else through your Twist sequence with minimal demonstration and without notes. If your volunteer cannot do all poses and transitions with stable ease, offer pose variations.
   h) Ask your volunteer for feedback in the following areas:
      What was their overall experience of class?
      What did they like best about your teaching?
      What is one thing they could tell you to help you grow?

3. Move

   Take a class labeled Revolved Poses. Before and after class, note sensations in your body.

   Before: My heart feels ___________, my head feels _________, my feet feel ___________.

   After: My heart feels ___________, my head feels _________, my feet feel ___________.

Inversions

Your mat is your lab.
The ultimate experiment is removing unhealthy aspects of ego from the formula.

Inversions are a category of poses that impact the components of your Nervous System via inverting your brain relative to your heart. They are also a great on-the-mat practice of Dharana, or laser focus because they involve hand placement, spinal alignment, core and bandha engagement, preparation, controlled breathing, specific relaxation points, and controlled ascents and descents. Inversions can strengthen the entire body, improve balance, boost positive energy, and heighten self-awareness so long as they are done safely. However, inversions can also expose parts of your ego still seeking to validate self-worth at the expense of your body and brain. Teachers who are informed, present and supportive can be a key part of the inversion formula. Important notes for inversions include:

- ✓ Serious injuries have occurred in big inversions, so modified practice is recommended first.
- ✓ It is recommended to learn big inversions with a knowledgeable teacher as these poses require preparation, energetic alignment, strength, engagement of bandhas and breathing techniques, focus, a well-timed confident descent, and intrinsic inspiration to have optimum benefit.
- ✓ Come out of an inversion in reverse steps of going in and always come out before the body is tired.
- ✓ Cautions presented cannot cover all variables and are not a substitute for medical advice.
- ✓ Variations are recommended for prenatal, osteoporosis, and conditions of the neck, eye, and heart.
- ✓ If a practitioner is without use of one or more limbs, modify variations to engage available joints.
- ✓ Additional Inversions (with variations) can be found in the Ashtanga Primary Sequence poses.
- ✓ Some Inversions are not provided in this book on purpose due to injury risks.

77. Extended Puppy - Uttana Shishosana (Uttana = Extended, Shisho = Puppy)

Chakras/Doshas/Vayus. Root, 3rd Eye/All/Upward, downward.

Cautions.　　Shoulder and knee conditions.

Benefits.　　Stretches upper back, spine, and shoulders. Can reduce tension.

Cues.　　From Table, walk hands forward, chest moves toward floor.

Shoulders broaden, forehead rests.

Hips and ribs draw in and upward to stabilize lower back.

Micro bend elbows, wide fingers press downward.

Sequence.　　Child's Pose, Table, Dolphin, Gate.

Variations.　　Lessen angle for shoulder and back support.

Stack forearms under forehead;

or rest on elbows with hands in prayer above neck.

Child's Pose.

78. Standing Seal - Dandayamana Yoga Mudrasana (Dandayamana = Standing, Mudra = Seal)

Chakras/Doshas/Vayus. Root, 3rd Eye/All/Downward, upward.

Cautions.　　Shoulder, heart, and eye conditions.

Benefits.　　Stretches back body. Can promote sense of heart-mind balance.

Cues.　　From Mountain, exhale step feet wider than hips.

Hands come low behind back, fingers interlocked.

Exhale to hinge forward from hips (micro-bend knees).

Hands engage upward; gaze between legs.

Sequence.　　Palm Tree, Tree, Squat, 5-Pointed Star, Goddess.

Variations.　　Bend elbows and interlock hands behind back.

Prone Child's Pose.

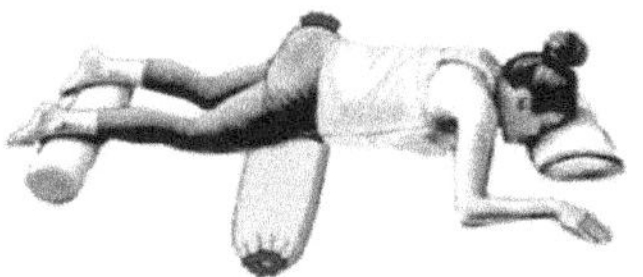

79. Rabbit – Sasangasana (Sasaka = Rabbit)

Chakras/Doshas/Vayus. 3rd Eye/All except Kapha Imbalance/Downward, upward.

Cautions.	Pre-natal, heart, eye, joint and back (neck too) conditions and osteoporosis.
Benefits.	Can stretch shoulders, arms, and back.
	Can reduce tension and promote intuition.
Cues.	From Table, lower top of head to floor.
	Hands reach toward feet and grasp heels.
	Tailbone is lifted, thighs perpendicular to floor.
	Head rests softly between shoulders.
	Natural arch in neck with face toward knees.
Sequence.	Baby, Camel, Child's Pose, Hero, Savasana.
Variations.	Baby Pose, hands at sides or near face.

80. Hand Stand (modified) - Adho Mukha Vrksa (Adho mukha = Face Downward; Vrksa = Tree)

Chakras/Doshas/Vayus. 3rd Eye/All/ Balancing, upward, expanding.

Cautions.	Pre-natal, heart, eye, joint and back conditions, and osteoporosis conditions.
Benefits.	Can strengthens entire body and improve balance.
	Can reduce stress, promote intuition and inner wisdom.
Cues.	From Dandasana with soles of feet on wall.
	Note hand position, turn body over.
	Place hands in same position at shoulder-width.
	Fingers spread; base of index fingers presses firmly.
	Broaden shoulder blades into back torso and toward tailbone.
	Rotate upper arms outward while energetically drawing inward.
	Place one heel at a time on wall at hip level (90 degrees to torso).
	Push through heels, engage core to stabilize hips over shoulders.
	Draw front ribs in, reach tailbone toward heels.
	Neutral head between shoulder blades with natural arch in neck.
	Loosen jaw and relax neck.
	Descend with core engaged and shoulder blades lifted/broad, one foot down at a time
Sequence.	Legs Up the Wall, Child's Pose, Snake, Savasana.
Variations.	Legs Up the Wall or Puppy.

Lions, Bears and Birds Oh My

As a student, you may hear some reference to matching your hand and foot placement to other poses for correct alignment in a new pose (i.e., Plank to Downward Facing Dog). While this is true in many bodies, it is not a true statement for others. According to Ayurveda, people are comprised primarily of one constitution out of three that are possible. Those three constitutions show up as different in physical presentation as would a lion (Pitta) standing next to a bird (Vata) who is standing next to a bear (Kapha). Though people can change parts of their shape through exercise and surgery, limb and torso lengths are what they are since birth.

Vatas often have longer arms and more lanky shape (like a bird). Kaphas have more dense structure in general (like a bear) with less leverage in limbs. Pittas typically have average limb lengths in relation to torso with more obvious muscular structure (like a lion). So, one size fits all hand and feet placement will never work. For example, in Handstand at the wall, one's hands may be further from or closer to the wall depending on torso and leg length and may be shoulder-width or a bit narrower depending on bone and muscular structure.

Similarly, the effort needed to hold handstands can be more relative to leverage and equanimity of limbs and torsos than it is a matter of perceived "toughness."

81. **Supported Head Stand** - **Salamba Sirsasana** (Sa=with, alamba=that on which one rests, sirsa=head)

Chakras/Doshas/Vayus. 3rd Eye/All/ Balancing, upward, expanding.

Cautions.	Pre-natal, heart, eye, joint/back conditions, osteoporosis.
Benefits.	Strengthens limbs and core; can improve balance.
	Can reduce stress; promotes intuition/inner wisdom.
Cues.	From Staff with soles of feet on wall, note hand position.
	Turn body over, place hands in same position for Dolphin.
	Adjust forearms width - clasp hands to opposite elbows to measure.
	Interlace fingers, flatten pinkies, place back of head at base of thumbs.
	Head is NOT weighted as feet walk in until hips are over shoulders.
	Press forearms downward while lifting out of the shoulders.
	Lift and place one heel at a time on wall at hip level (90 degrees to torso).
	Draw ribs in, tailbone toward heels, engage core to stabilize hips over shoulders.
	Neutral head between shoulder blades, natural arch in neck, loosen jaw, relax neck.
	Descend with core engaged and shoulder blades lifted, one foot at a time.
Sequence.	Child's Pose, Bridge, Savasana.
Variations.	Dolphin Pose.
	Legs Up the Wall.
	Extend one leg at a time upward.

82. Legs Up the Wall - Viparita Karani (Viparita = Reversed, Karani = In Action)

Chakras/Doshas/Vayus. 3rd Eye, Throat/All/Upward, downward.

Cautions.   Heart and eye conditions.

Benefits.   Stretches back, hamstrings and shoulders. Can reduce tension.

Cues.   Sit next to wall with right side of body touching wall, lower back to ground.

Rotate pelvis and lift legs so backs of legs are against wall, arms open to sides.

Sequence.   Happy Baby, Spinal Twist, Savasana.

Variations.   Legs up with hands supporting legs.

Place blanket or bolster under hips and torso.

Practice

1. Breathe

Review Surya Bhedana, Chandra Bhedana, and Nadi Shodhana breathing techniques. Practice each breath for 1-3 minutes, allowing long breaks between them. Then lead someone else through these breaths.

2. Experiment, Create and Teach

    a) Review the new inversions in this section, as well as previous inversions in the Ashtanga Primary Series (most are in the Finishing Series). Practice this section's inversions, starting from the variations lowest to the ground and working upward, along with counterposes for spinal stability in between each.

    b) Choose 2-3 Inversions with low variations that support heightened self-awareness over ego.

    c) Choose 2-3 counterposes to stabilize the spine between Inversions (see pose Sequence ideas).

    d) Choose 1 channel activating breath that supports a sense of Nervous System balance for you.

    e) Draft a 20-minute Inversion sequence that includes inversions, low variations, counterposes and complimentary breathing techniques in a fluid sequence offering unhurried/equal time for each.

    f) Review your sequence for equanimity in joints and muscles, and for the health condition you are most interested in to adjust your sequence accordingly.

    g) Lead someone else your Inversion sequence with minimal demonstration and without notes. If your volunteer cannot do all poses and transitions with ease, offer pose variations.

    h) Ask your volunteer for feedback in the following areas:

    What was their overall experience of class?

    What did they like best about your teaching?

    What is one thing they could tell you to help you grow?

3. Move

Take a yoga class labeled as Inversions. Before and after class, note sensations in your body.

Before: My heart feels ___________, my head feels __________, my feet feel ___________.

After:　My heart feels ___________, my head feels __________, my feet feel ___________.

Yin

Question everything.
Then drop in to that place inside you where ancient wisdom lies.
And the truth comes.

Yin is a relatively modern practice with origins in Taoist principles and Traditional Chinese Medicine. The formulization of practices into Yin began with Paulie Zink, who in the 1980s taught a combination of Hatha Yoga with Taoist Yoga. One of Zink's students was Paul Grilley who went on to study with Hiroshi Motoyama, a Japanese scholar and yogi who focused on the physiology of the meridians and the qi (or Chi). Grilley went on to develop Yin sequences with aims similar to an acupuncturist – targeted stress along meridian pathways.

In Yin yoga, Yin is associated with moon energy that is stable, immobile, feminine, passive, cold, and downward movement that relates to the connective tissues (tendons, ligaments, fascia). The practice of Yin targets connective tissues in a relatively cool body and environment to cultivate internal spaciousness. Yin is also a form of Pratyahara, control of distractions for a sense of increased personal autonomy.

A classical Yin practice occurs before the body is warmed. If muscles are warm and/or poses are held briefly, you are in the world of Yang - associated with the sun, or energy that is mobile, masculine, active, hot, and upward movement relating to muscles and blood. Sometimes, Yin poses show up in short durations in a warm body as part of a practice; however, this method does not constitute Yin practice.

Practitioners may confuse Yin practice with Restorative yoga, which is something entirely different. Restorative yoga utilizes props and comfort as paramount to mind-body relaxation. Yin does not typically use props or even emphasize comfort, in fact Yin practice that targets connective tissue is often not comfortable in general, though it can be very meditative.

From an Ayurvedic perspective, Yin is not generally beneficial for those with a lot of Vata or Kapha (people with more air/flexibility in their joints or earth energy/slowness of metabolism), so Yin is most beneficial as a counter to Yang, or heat (Pitta constitution or Pitta excess). As with all practices, however, one's individual health history must be considered. Some important notes for Yin poses include:

- ✓ Moving between Yin postures must be done slowly so as not to break the connective tissue.
- ✓ Yin poses, done in accordance with Yin principles, include long holds (usually at least 3 minutes).
- ✓ Yin poses can cause injury, especially in those who are naturally very flexible or have degenerative changes in their joints and bones.
- ✓ Cautions presented cannot cover all variables and are not a substitute for medical advice.
- ✓ Fusing Yin practice with vinyasa is not recommended due to risk of connective tissue damage.
- ✓ Yin pose variations that include props are recommended for Yin poses not used in a Yin practice.
- ✓ Variations are recommended for prenatal, osteoporosis, and joint conditions.
- ✓ If a practitioner is without use of one or more limbs, modify variations to engage available joints.
- ✓ Some Yin poses are not provided in this book on purpose due to injury risks.

83. Butterfly – Baddha Konasana (Baddha = Bound, Kona = Angle)

Chakras/Doshas/Vayus. Root, Sacral/All/Downward.

Cautions.	Osteoporosis, knee, sciatica, and back conditions.
Benefits.	Stimulates kidney, liver, bladder, and spleen.
	Can improve flexibility, ease tension, and promote sleep.
Cues.	From Easy Pose, bring soles of feet together, knees wide.
	Press feet away to create diamond shape with legs.
	Inhale to lengthen spine, exhale hinge forward over feet.
	Hands and forehead rest on floor.
	Suggested hold time is 5 minutes.
Sequence.	Deer, Cowface, Frog.
Variations.	Torso stays upright with hands to thighs and/or tailbone on bolster.
	Legs Up the Wall with variation of leg and feet.
	Reclining Bound Angle.

84. Deer - Paschimottanasana (Paschima = West, Uttan = Intense)

Chakras/Doshas/Vayus. Root, Sacral/All/Downward.

Cautions.	Pre-natal, osteoporosis, knee, and back conditions.
Benefits.	Stimulates liver and kidneys.
	Can improve flexibility and ease mental tension.
Cues.	From Butterfly, bring one leg behind body.
	Move both feet away from hips, sit bones stay grounded.
	Front shin is parallel to back thigh; both feet are flexed.
	Inhale arms up, lengthen spine, exhale fold over front leg, forearms to floor.
	Shoulders, head and neck are neutral and relaxed.
	Suggested hold time each side is 3 minutes.
Sequence.	Sphynx, Dragon, Spinal Twist.
Variations.	Torso remains more upright, or bolster under torso with head elevated by a block.
	Reverse Pigeon
	Fallen Deer, perform one leg at a time while laying on abdomen.

85. Sphynx - Salamba Bhujangasana (Salamba = Supported, Bhujang = Snake or Cobra)

Chakras/Doshas/Vayus. Root, Sacral, Heart/All except Kapha Imbalance/Inward, downward.

Cautions.	Pre-natal, osteoporosis, and back conditions.
Benefits.	Stimulates bladder, kidney, stomach, spleen, and adrenals.
	Can ease back and pelvic pain and promote clarity.
Cues.	Lay on stomach, legs straight, lift chest and head, place elbows under shoulders.
	Forearms and hands are parallel and press downward.
	Lower back broadens and lengthens toward heels.
	Navel draws upward as collarbones broaden.
	Head stacks over shoulders, gaze forward.
	Suggested hold time is 3 minutes.
Sequence.	Deer, Cowface, Frog.
Variations.	Slide elbows further away to reduce spinal compression.
	Bolster under chest and shoulders for arm support.

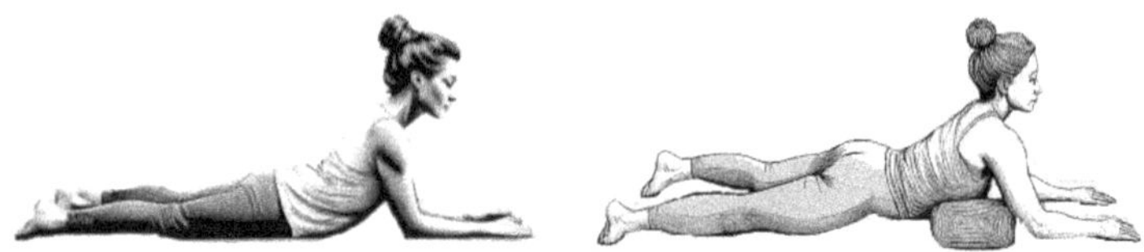

86. Dragon - Utthan Pristhasana (Uttha = Intense, Pristha = Lizard)

Chakras/Doshas/Vayus. Root, Sacral/All/ Downward, balancing.

Cautions.	Pre-natal, knee, and ankle conditions.
Benefits.	Stimulates kidney, liver, spleen, stomach, and gallbladder.
	Can decrease hip and back tension and promote positivity.
Cues.	From Table, step right foot between hands.
	Right knee aligns over right heel.
	Left knee and leg slide backward for thigh stretch.
	Torso is active over hands, not resting or sinking.
	Suggested hold time is 3 minutes per side.
Sequence.	Twisted Dragon, Lizard, Balancing Table, Gate.
Variations.	Keep torso upright, hands on thigh (Dragon Flying High).
	Bring forearms down to floor (Lizard) or to blocks.
	Place right hand inside right knee, revolve torso to right, gaze upward (Twisted Dragon).

87. Cowface - Gomukhasana (Go = Cow, Mukha = Face)

Chakras/Doshas/Vayus. Root, Sacral/All/ Inward, downward, balancing.

Cautions.	Osteoporosis, shoulder, knee, and ankle conditions.
Benefits.	Stimulates heart and bladder meridians.
	Can increase hip/shoulder mobility and sense of inner stability.
Cues.	From Table, cross knees by bringing left leg in front of right leg.
	Lean backward to sit.
	Raise and bend right elbow, place hand between shoulder blades.
	Bend left elbow low behind back so hand can grasp right hand.
	Inhale to lengthen spine, exhale hinge forward over feet.
	Suggested hold time is 3 minutes per side.
Sequence.	Frog, Bow, Supine Twist.
Variations.	Perform arms portion of pose only.
	Sit on a block to elevate hips, place strap between hands.
	Perform legs only portion of pose (Shoelace).

88. Frog - Mandukasana (Manduk = Frog)

Chakras/Doshas/Vayus. Root, Sacral/All except Kapha Imbalance/Downward, balancing.

Cautions.	Pre-natal, osteoporosis, back, hip and knee conditions.
Benefits.	Stimulates liver, kidney, and spleen meridians.
	Can ease back and pelvic pain and promote clarity.
Cues.	From Table, widen space between knees.
	Flex feet, toes out, heels and knees aligned.
	Walk hands forward to forearms.
	Abdomen is lifted; top of head is forward.
	Suggested hold time is 5 minutes.
Sequence.	Sphinx, Baby, Rabbit.
Variations.	Keep torso more upright, knees closer together, feet angled inward or neutral, and place bolster under chest.

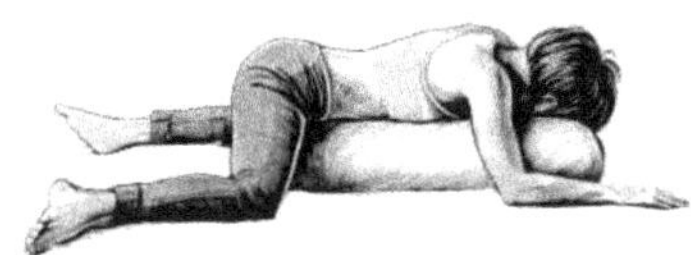

Practice

1. Breathe

Review Sitali, Whistle and Humming Breaths. Practice each breath for 1-3 minutes, though give yourself some time in between each or your blood pressure may change too dramatically. Then lead someone through these breaths.

2. Create and Teach
    a) Review the Yin poses and practice each Yin pose and version.
    b) Choose 3 Yin poses and a cooling breath that you feel most support a sense of increased physical spaciousness and personal autonomy for you.
    c) Draft a 15-minute Yin sequence that includes Yin poses, careful transitions and your breathing technique in a fluid sequence that offers unhurried and equal time for each.
    d) Lead someone else through your Yin sequence with minimal demonstration and without notes. If your volunteer cannot do all poses without injury, offer pose variations.
    e) Ask your volunteer for feedback in the following areas:

    What was their overall experience of class?

    What did they like best about your teaching?

    What is one thing they could tell you to help you grow?

3. Move

Take a class labeled as Yin. Before and after class, note sensations in your body.

Before: My heart feels ___________, my head feels _________, my feet feel ___________.

After: My heart feels __________, my head feels _________, my feet feel __________.

Kundalini

I am love, I am light, all the things.
And I am human.
and it is fucking hard.
so I clean the volcano.

Kundalini is considered the Yoga of Awareness and is associated with Laya yoga, the Yoga of Absorption. Kundalini and Laya yoga involve Tantric philosophy of energy movement, mantra, and meditative absorption.

In the late 1960s, Yogi Bhajan introduced a distinct form of Kundalini yoga to California as a combination of Bhakti and Raja yoga including mantra, poses, breathing techniques, and mudras. Bhajan's Kundalini teachings, however, included mantras in Gurmukh, a script associated with Sikh sacred texts, which differs from Laya mantras that are primarily in Sanskrit. After his death in 2004, awareness of abuses committed by Yogi Bhajan revealed that his behaviors were not in alignment with yogic of Sikh ethics. As a result, many of his teachings were revised in an effort to preserve valuable practices without perpetuating harm.

Kundalini kriyas are set sequences (poses, breathing, mudras, meditations, and mantras) for desired outcomes. Kundalini's focus on both nadi (yoga's energetic pathways) and interpretive meridians (TCM's energetic pathways), so kriyas can appeal to those desiring heightened control of outcomes. For example, there are kriyas for the nervous system, endocrine system, etc., and kundalini movements are sometimes incorporated into neurological and integrative health programs. Some important notes for Kundalini practices are:

✓ There are hundreds of kundalini kriyas, this section provided only a small sample.

✓ Radiance Charger, Stretch Pose, Archer Warrior, and Frog poses outlined separately here are provided as examples of using Kundalini poses outside of kriyas to keep things fresh in sequences.

✓ Parts of kriyas in this section are modified for accessibility and functional health purposes.

✓ Further variations are recommended for those with high blood pressure, glaucoma, heart conditions, history of seizures/stroke, intake of psychedelics, and those pregnant or menstruating.

✓ Cautions presented cannot cover all variables and are not a substitute for medical advice.

✓ Seated kriyas can be performed standing or in a chair. Though some energetics will shift due to location of spine in relation to grounding, it may be the only way to receive similar kriya benefits.

✓ To modify kriya times, apply changes to kriya parts as a percentage, so equation remains the same.

✓ When taking breaks, continue energetics by imagining yourself doing it, then return when ready.

✓ Indoctrination that kriyas must be as taught by Bhajan can limit awareness of personal experience.

IMPACT OF TIME IN PRACTICE

Below is a guideline for how durations of time may have differing benefits according to some Kundalini teachings. Minutes of time apply to how long you do one mantra or breathing technique or kriya. Days of time apply to how many days in a row you do a specific kriya, mantra, or breathing technique. For example, a 40-day sadhana includes practicing a specific kriya for desired outcome for 40 days in a row.

3 min	Increased circulation can be felt.
7 min	Brain begins to shift to alpha waves.
11 min	Pituitary and glandular system chemicals shift towards homeostasis.
22 min	Thoughts that are negative, positive, and neutral come into harmony.
31 min	A sense of alignment radiates from within and lasts throughout the day.
11 days	The # of infinity, breaking free starts, binds loosen.
21 days	A shift occurs of inwardly stepping back from unhealthy habits.
40 days	A break from demoting habits can be experienced.
90 days	A new promoting habit is established in your conscious and unconscious.
120 days	Your system harmonizes in such a way you may feel unfuckable.
1000 days	The positive shift in your life can be beyond your present comprehension.

*Please note that many kriyas require countering practices for functional wellness.

89. Radiance Charger (Also called Ego Eradicator)

Chakras/Doshas/Vayus. Heart, Crown/All/ Inward, expanding.

Cautions. Pre-natal, heavy menstruation, and shoulder conditions.

Benefits. Can stimulate lungs, spark a radiant glow, and inspire clarity.

Cues. Lift and extend arms 60 degrees from torso.

Arms/elbows are straight, shoulder blades lower into upper back.

Palms wide, thumbs up, fingers curl in pressing on knuckle pads.

Erect spine, internal focus above head, begin Breath of Fire

Suggested time is 1-3 minutes.

To finish, inhale as thumbs touch overhead. Exhale release arms.

Sequence. Meditation, Rabbit, Savasana.

Variations. Perform while standing or seated.

Other variations are limited

(angle of armpits activates lymphatics/heart meridian, fingers activate pressure points).

90. Stretch Pose

Chakras/Doshas/Vayus. Solar/All/Inward, balancing, expanding.

Cautions. Pre-natal, start of menstruation, neck, and lower back conditions.

Benefits. Can strengthen core, stimulate reproductive organs, and boost confidence.

Cues. Lay on back, legs are straight, toes point away from torso.

Arms are straight, palms face but don't touch legs.

Elongate body from feet to top of head.

Inhale to lift shoulders, neck, head, hands, legs, and feet about 6" off ground.

Begin Breath of Fire, gaze toward toes.

Suggested time is 1-3 minutes.

Sequence. Bridge, Happy Baby, Spinal Twist.

Variations. Bend one knee at a time,

bent knee foot on the ground and/or cradle head with hands.

Place blanket under feet and/or head for support.

One of These Things Are Not Like the Other

Kriya poses sometimes look like other Hatha poses but have different names; or don't look anything like other Hatha poses with the same names. Examples of these poses in Kundalini are Rock, Archer, Frog, Spinal Flex, etc. While these similarities and differences can be confusing, actually Kundalini's naming conventions make a lot of sense. For example, Kundalini Frog pose is different than how frog pose is practiced in Yin, but both are frogs. Kundalini's Frog just looks like it is jumping over lily pads. When practicing Kundalini's Frog, take variations offered if experiencing any issues in SI joints, lower back, knees, and ankles . . . or you might end up feeling like a flattened frog.

91. Archer Pose (Also called Archer Warrior or Hero Posture)

Chakras/Doshas/Vayus. Solar, Heart /All/ Inward, balancing, expanding.

Cautions. Unnaturally angling hips on "railroad tracks" reduces pelvic stability.

Benefits. Stretches hips, groin, chest and strengthens legs, back, arms.
Can increase stamina.

Cues. From Warrior II, turn thumbs up,
Other fingers curl inward pressing knuckle pads.
Bend back elbow, draw hand toward armpit, like pulling a bow.
Gaze over front thumb. begin Breath of Fire.
Suggested time is 3-11 minutes each side.
To finish, inhale take aim, then Cannon exhale.

Sequence. Star, Plank, Reverse Warrior.

Variations. Lessen width and depth of stance or perform in chair.

92. Frog

Chakras/Doshas/Vayus. Sacral/All except Vata Imbalance/ Inward, upward, downward, expanding.

Cautions. Pre-natal, ankle, knee, hip, lower back, and heart conditions.

Benefits. Can stimulate endocrine/circulatory systems and improve energy.
Stretches pelvic muscles and can strengthen quadriceps and feet.

Cues. Squat with fingers to floor, feet together; rotate and lift feet so heels touch.
Inhale broaden collarbones, gaze forward, like a frog ready to leap.
Exhale to straight knees, folding forward, nose to knees.
Breath is forceful inhales and exhales through the nose.
Suggested time is 26 repetitions or 3-5 minutes.

Sequence. Mini-savasana, Bridge, Reverse Plank.

Variations. Inhale Goddess, Exhale Wide-Legged Forward Fold.
In chair, inhale Goddess, exhale Forward Bend.
On block, inhale Squat, exhale Forward Bend to block.
Inhale Reclining Cow to and exhale hug knees to chest.

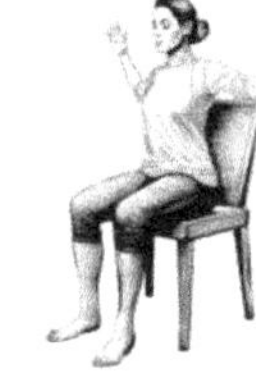

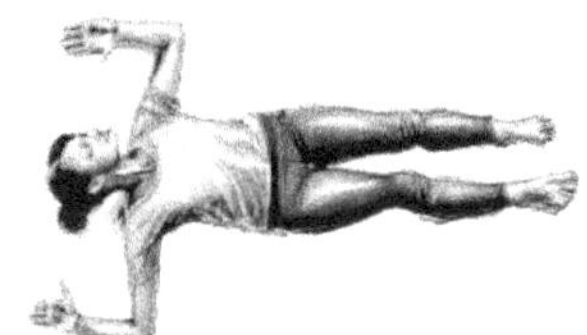
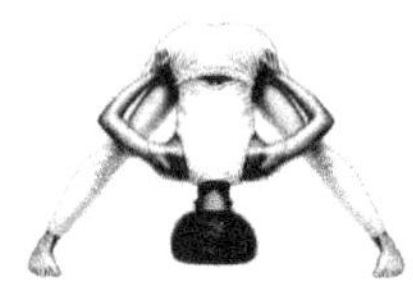

93. Spinal Energy Activation Kriya

Chakras/Doshas/Vayus. All/All/All.

Cautions.   Pre-natal, heart, back, hip, knee, ankle, shoulder, and wrist conditions.

Benefits.   Can increase spinal flexibility/circulation. Stimulates chakras for heightened well-being.

Sequence.   Near end of class followed by Savasana and/or Mantra.

Cues.   Breaths are quick/forceful through nose, except slow/gentle for neck rolls.

a.   Spine Flex Low, 2 minutes.

Easy Pose, hands on ankles, inhale arch low spine forward, exhale round spine, chin level.

b.   Spine Flex Middle, 2 minutes.

Hero Pose, hands on thighs, inhale arch mid-spine forward, exhale round, chin level.

c.   Washing Machine, 2 minutes.

Easy Pose, hands on shoulders (fingers front/thumbs back), elbows straight out to sides, inhale twist left, exhale twist right.

d.   Bear Grip Turn, 2 minutes.

Easy Pose, grip fingers at chest (left palm faces out), inhale left elbow up as right elbow goes down, exhale right elbow up as left elbow goes down, hands rotate at center.
Variation – hands on top of one another at heart center.

e.   Upper Spine Flex, 2 minutes.

Easy Pose, hands on knees, arms straight, inhale arch forward, exhale round, chin level.

f.   Shoulder Shrugs, 1 minute.

Easy Pose, hands on knees, inhale shoulders up toward ears, exhale lower shoulders.

g.   Neck Rolls, 1 minute.

Easy Pose, hands on knees, inhale left ear toward left shoulder, exhale to roll neck to right side through front, motion/breath is slow.

h.   Bear Grip Lock, 3 times.

Easy Pose, elbows bend to grip fingers at throat level (left palm out), inhale to suspend in breath and pull lock, then exhale to suspend out breath. Bring grip overhead, inhale to suspend in breath and pull lock overhead, then exhale to suspend out breath. Engage Mula bandh when breath suspended. Variation – grasp opposite forearms.

i.   Sat Kriya, 3 to 7 minutes.

Hero, clasp hands overhead, index fingers up, elbows straight, inhale Sat, exhale Nam. Variation engage Uddiyana bandh on inhale, release on exhale, clasped hands on head.

j.   Mini Savasana, 2-5 minutes.

94. Pittra Kriya

Chakras/Doshas/Vayus. Heart, Throat, 3rd Eye/All/All.

Cautions. Kriya's recommended durations of 11 minutes are reduced due to shoulder injury risk.

If practicing this kriya for 40 days, alternate arms when throwing water to reduce risks.

Benefits. Throwing water stimulates the endocrine system.

Shuni mudra and Har stimulates meridians to pituitary (master gland).

Superman stimulates parasympathetic and sympathetic nervous systems.

Sequence. Savasana, Meditation, Cowface.

Cues. Use strong inhales/exhales through nose, except when chanting Har.

a. Throwing Water, 3 minutes.

Easy Pose, left hand on heart, right arm bent by side, palm cupped.

Lift right hand to "throw water" over shoulder (wrist crosses ear).

Gaze at nose. To finish, do next step 3 times.

With right hand over shoulder, inhale suspend breath 15 seconds, then exhale.

b. Shuni Mudra, 3 minutes.

Easy Pose, elbows bent near ribcage, forearms held straight to hands at 45-degree angle out from sides, hands are higher than elbows.

Curl middle fingers in so thumbs press middle fingernails (Shuni mudra).

Flick thumb/middle finger, chant "Har" as tongue strikes roof of mouth (sounds like Hud). Gaze at nose. To finish, do next step 3 times.

Inhale, suspend breath while flicking for 15 seconds, then Cannon exhale.

c. Superman Pose, 3 minutes.

Easy Pose, form "V" with straight arms at throat level, hands flat with fingers "plugged in", palms down. At 1 time/second, cross hands (alternate hand crossing on top), chant Har with tongue strikes to roof of mouth. Gaze at nose. To finish, do next step 3 times.

Inhale, suspend breath, cross arms fast 10 seconds, Cannon exhale.

The Great Unraveling

Choosing a kriya for 40 days of practice can be daunting, partly because there are many kriyas to choose from, but also because doing strange movements over and over can be challenging for both mind and body. According to timelines at the start of this section, if a kriya is practiced for 40 days, habits can be broken. But what else might show up broken (i.e., connective tissue)? This conundrum becomes easier with the guidance of a Kundalini teacher who is aware of your desired outcome and understands anatomy.

Once a kriya is chosen and modifications are outlined by one who grasps kriya technology and functional movement, then the rest is up to the practitioner's determination. Some teachers warn that if one day out of 40 days is missed, you must begin again. While this 40-day streak can have potent rewards, Kundalini is the yoga of awareness and essentially that awareness comes from within. The greatest unraveling of a repetitive kriya is the exposure of complex emotions and realizations. When you stop experiencing revelations, the kriya has likely helped you bring suffering to the surface where it can at last release its negative grip . . . though this release can be temporary without also doing other relevant work.

95. Surya Kriya

Chakras/Doshas/Vayus. Root, Sacral, Solar Plexus/All/ All.

Cautions. Pre-natal, heart, shoulder, knee, hip, and ankle conditions.

Benefits. Right Nostril breathing promotes clarity and focus.

Sat Kriya promotes heightened sense of well-being.

Spinal Flex increases spinal lubrication and flexibility.

Frog stimulates reproductive organs.

Neck Turns open throat and stimulate thyroid.

Qigong Feathers stretches shoulders and arms and balances energy.

Meditation promotes healthy brain activity (clarity, memory, focus, sleep, etc.).

Sequence. Meditation, Mantra, Sun Salutations, Savasana.

Cues. Strong inhales and exhales through the nose, except when chanting.

a. Right nostril breathing, 2.5 minutes.

Easy Pose, right arm straight, hand on knee in Gyan mudra. Block left nostril with left thumb, other left hand fingers straight up. Inhale and exhale right nostril only.

b. Sat Kriya, 6 minutes.

Rock Pose, clasp hands overhead, index fingers up, elbows straight, inhale Sat, exhale Nam. Internal gaze to 3rd Eye. At 3 min, inhale to suspend breath, engage Mula bandh, then relax. Repeat at end. Variation – Inhale Uddiyana, release bandh on exhale, clasped hands on head.

c. Spinal Flex, 1.5 minutes.

Easy Pose, hands on ankles, inhale arch spine forward, exhale round spine, chin stays level. Apply Mula bandh on exhales. To finish, inhale, suspend breath, then relax.

d. Frog pose, 30 seconds or 26 repetitions.

Squat, bring feet together, lift heels, bring heels to touch. Fingers on floor, collarbones and chest wide, gaze forward. Inhale ready to leap, exhale to straight knees in Forward Bend, one repetition is complete. See more variations listed under Frog Pose.

e. Neck Turns, 1.5 minutes.

Hero/Rock pose with straight spine and hands on thighs, inhale head left ("Sat" - inner voice), exhale head right ("Nam" - inner voice). To finish, head comes to neutral.

f. Modified Qigong Spreading Feathers (in place of Spinal Bend), 1.5 minutes.

Easy Pose, inhale arms to sides with elbows slightly bent, thumbs up, exhale to lower thumbs down, lower one arm at a time. Spinal Bend removed due to injury risk to spine.

g. Meditation, 3-31 minutes.

From Easy Pose, spine straight, arms straight, backs of wrists on knees, Gyan mudra, "Sat" with inner voice on inhales, "Nam" with inner voice on exhales.

96. Reboot Kriya (Modified) (Also called Kriya for the Lymph Glands)

Chakras/Doshas/Vayus. All/All/Inward, downward, balancing, elevating, and expanding.

Cautions. Pre-natal, heavy menstruation, heart, shoulder, hip, knee, and ankle conditions.

Some poses from the original kriya (bicycle, shoulder stand bicycle, plow scissors, Har guru chant, Har guru bowing) are modified for functional wellness purposes.

Benefits. Spinal Twist stimulates digestive meridians.

Push Pull stimulates lymph glands.

Lion's Roar boosts immune system.

Arm Pumps help balance nervous system.

Frog Pose stimulates reproductive organs.

Table Kicks increase circulation.

Radiance Charger stimulates radiance and inspires clarity.

Sequence. Savasana or Mantra (try the Bliss mantra).

Cues. Use Breath of Fire or Ujjayi, except during Lion's Roar.

a. Twist on Spinal Twist, 3 minutes.

Easy Pose, fingers on top of head, thumbs close ears, elbows lift and stay upward, inhale to twist left, exhale center, inhale twist right, exhale center (4 motions).

b. Push Pull, 3 minutes.

Easy Pose, thumbs press base of pinky fingers, palms up. Elbows bend near ribs, hands at shoulder level face sides. Inhale to straighten left arm up at 60-degree angle, exhale left arm back to start as right arm goes up at 60-degree angle. Alternate hands up and down in a push-pull motion. Variation – divide movement into 4 parts to slow it down.

c. Lion's Roar, 3 minutes

Easy Pose, hands on knees, palms up like lion's claw. Shape mouth like an "O," inhale loudly as arms lift overhead, exhale through "O" mouth loudly as hands return to knees. See Lion's Roar breathing technique for other variations.

d. Arm Pumps, 3 minutes.

Hands in fists, thumbs under fingers, arms straight out to sides.

Palm down, inhale arms up 20 degrees, inhale up another 20 degrees, exhale lower 20 degrees, exhale lower again 20 degrees. 4-part movement (quick, separate, rhythmical).

e. Frog Pose, 3 minutes. See earlier pose cues and other variations.

f. Table Kicks, 1.5 minutes each side.

From Table, inhale gaze up and extend right foot back foot like a kick, exhale Cat as knee bends and returns to Table. Variation – standing alternate knee (heel to buttocks).

g. Radiance Charger, 3 minutes. See earlier pose cues.

To finish, inhale, suspend, thumbs touch overhead, exhale and release.

97. Elementary Stress Kriya (Also called Relieving Your Elementary Stress)

Chakras/Doshas/Vayus. Heart, Throat, 3rd Eye/All/ Downward, balancing, expanding.

Cautions. Shoulder and wrist conditions.

Benefits. Clap Sequence promotes primal thinking homeostasis.

Elbow Bounce stimulates acupoints to reduce pain.

Criss Cross Hands promotes left and right brain balance.

Hand Drums ease stress and promote creativity.

Dance stimulates positive chemistry and cognitive function.

Heart Meditation promotes effortless clarity. Mantra can elevate awareness.

Sequence. After active portion of class and prior to release portion of class.

Cues. Use strong inhales and exhales through nose during first 3 movements.

a. Clap Sequence, 4 minutes.

Easy Pose, fingers of hands engage as one unit, palms are flat, repeat:

1. Slap thighs twice with palms.
2. Clap hands in front of chest.
3. Open hands in V (option to tap sides of hands together).
4. Clap hands in front of chest again.

At 3 minutes in, inhale and suspend breath, then exhale. Clap again for 1 minute.

b. Elbow Bounce, 3 minutes.

Easy Pose, elbows bent, hands clasp at chest level with thumbs crossed, elbows bounce on ribcage sides. To finish, inhale, suspend 10 seconds, squeeze sides with elbows, exhale.

c. Criss-Cross Hands, 2.5 minutes

From Easy Pose, elbows relaxed, fingers wide, hands in front of shoulders, palms forward, criss cross hands in front of face using forearms. To finish, inhale and suspend 10 seconds, exhale.

d. Hand Drums, 3.5 minutes.

Easy Pose, shirt torso slightly forward and drum ground in front with hands, eyes closed, follow internal guide for rhythm. Variation – sit erect, bring hands to lap, or on thighs.

e. Dance, 3.5 minutes

Easy Pose, move torso, bounce shoulders and arms, dance. Variation – stand up to allow torso to move more freely. Original kriya dance time is 7 minutes.

f. Heart Meditation, 4 minutes

Easy Pose, left hand palm flat on chest center, right hand palm over left, eyes closed and mind relaxed. Original meditation time is 8.5 minutes.

g. Mantra or Affirmation, 1 minute.

Choose mantra or self-illuminating affirmation. The kriya suggests Chattr Chakkr Varti.

98. **Kriya for Energy** (also called Maiden Kriya and Workout for the Elementary Being)

Chakras/Doshas/Vayus. Solar, Heart, Throat/All except excess Vata or Pitta/All

Cautions.   Heart, pre-natal, shoulder, back, hip, and knee conditions.

Benefits.   Har strikes 34th, 35th, 36th meridians to stimulate pituitary gland.

Heel Drops stimulate osteoblasts for bone health.

Overhead Clap promotes immunity and positivity.

Ground Strike eases anxiety.

Arm Flaps stimulate lymphatics.

Criss-Cross Jumps promote circulation. Archer Pose increases stamina.

Backward Stretch activates the lymphatic system.

Side Stretch improves spinal flexibility and aids in digestion.

Adding heel drops with each movement can further promote bone density.

Sequence.   Qigong Laughter, as an Edge, or anytime to increase energy.

Cues.   Use Har chant, or forceful inhales and exhales.

Do each movement 8x while chanting Har (tongue strikes roof of mouth on "r").

When finished with a full round, start over. Repeat set for 5 to 12 minutes.

a.   Overhead Clap, 8 claps. Feet hip width apart, reach arms overhead to clap.

b.   Ground Strike. 8 strikes. Feet hip width apart, hinge forward to strike ground (or thighs).

c.   Arm Flaps, 8 flaps. Feet hip width apart, arms straight to sides parallel to ground, palms down, fingers "plugged in," raise and lower arms about 1 foot like flying.

d.   Criss-Cross Jumps, 8 crosses. Feet hip width apart, hop feet to cross in front as hands cross in front, alternate which foot and hand crosses on top. Variation – heel drops, cross only arms.

e.   Archer Pose, 8 pulses. See earlier pose cues.

Do both sides. To move to other side, inhale Star, exhale Archer Pose other side.

f.   Repeat Criss-Cross Jumps, 8 crosses.

g.   Backward Stretch, 8 pulses. Feet hip width apart, reach arms overhead, palms face out/up, arch back to gaze up and lean hands back. Variation – cactus arms like Cow.

h.   Repeat Criss-Cross Jumps, 8 crosses.

i.   Side Stretches, 4 pulses left and 4 pulses right.

Feet hip width apart, reach arms overhead, palms face forward or toward one another, lean left 4 pulses, then right 4 pulses. Variation – hands to shoulders.

j.   Repeat Criss-Cross Jumps, 8 crosses.

99. Subagh Kriya (also called Kriya for Gratitude or Kriya for Prosperity)

Chakras/Doshas/Vayus. Solar Plexus, Heart, Throat/All/ All.

Cautions.   Heart and shoulder conditions.

Benefits.   Hand Tap stimulates digestive and emotional regulation.

Hand Crosses promote balance in left and right brain.

Cheerleader stimulates digestive, respiratory, and immune system health.

Heart Navel Highway energizes feeling of confidence and unconditional love.

Jeannie balances heart energy in torso and promotes a sense of fulfillment.

Sequence.   As a closing, shorten to Hand Taps, Cheerleader, and Jeannie, each for 1 minute.

This kriya is a great wake-up call to energized gratitude anytime throughout the day.

Cues.   If not chanting, use strong and short inhales and exhales, except for Jeannie.

Pose names below are nicknames, not official names for these poses.

   a.   Hand Tap, 3 minutes.

Easy Pose, bend elbows, hands in front of chest, palms down.

Tap hand sides, thumbs cross underneath, then flip hands to tap pinky fingers.

Repeat in rhythmic/strong action while chanting Har

(tongue strikes roof of mouth on "r").

   b.   Hand Crosses, 3 minutes.

Easy Pose, arms up with elbows straight and fingers wide, palms forward.

Criss-cross hands, alternating top hand.

Variation – bend elbows to cross hands at a lower level in front of heart.

   c.   Cheerleader, 3 minutes.

Easy Pose, extend arms up from shoulders at 60 degrees, elbows are straight.

Press thumbs into palms, curl other fingers over thumbs into tight fists.

Move fists in small circles backwards, chanting Har.

   d.   Heart Navel Highway, 3 minutes.

Easy Pose, elbows bent, palms face abdomen without touching body,

palms are stacked with space between palms, fingers are straight in one solid unit.

Forearms to fingers remain straight as one hand moves upward while other hand lowers

to create energy highway from heat created by hands.

Chant Har Haray Haree, Whahay Guroo (or any that inspires universal bliss).

   e.   Jeannie, 3 minutes.

Easy Pose, elbows bent, forearms stacked right over left in front of chest,

1-minute breath (inhale 20 seconds, suspend 20 seconds, exhale 20 seconds).

Practice

1. Energy Circuits

   Review Breath of Fire. Practice for 3 minutes. Then ask someone to let you guide this breath.

2. Experiment, Create and Teach
   a) Choose a Kundalini kriya to teach someone else.
   b) List some poses, breathing, mantra, meditations, and gazes that support your kriya's intention.
   c) Draft a 30–60-minute sequence that includes your kriya and supportive poses, breathing techniques, mantras, meditations, and gazes. Remember kriya sequence is already set and if you change time for one of the kriya's poses or techniques, change time to other parts of the kriya in a similar ratio.
   d) Review your sequence for vayu directions, equanimity in joints and muscles, counter poses necessary, and for the health condition you are most interested in to make adjustments and/or add variations.
   e) Ask someone to let you lead them through your Kundalini class. Stop at any pose not working for your student and find one of the options of that pose that works and provides maximum benefit.
   f) Ask your volunteer for feedback in the following areas:
      What was their overall experience of class?
      What did they like best about your teaching?
      What is one thing they could tell you to help you grow?

3. Move

   Take a physical yoga class that includes a kriya from this section that supports an endocrine condition you are interested in. Before and after class, note sensations in these areas of your body.
      Before: My heart feels ___________, my head feels _________, my feet feel ___________.
      After: My heart feels ___________, my head feels _________, my feet feel ___________.

4. Mantra

   Experiment chanting the Magnificent mantra or another affirmation that promotes inner guidance.

Nidra

"We are here to awaken from our illusion of separateness" – Thich Nhat Hanh.

Yoga Nidra, a yogic practice typically done in Savasana, has been around since about 1000 BCE and is derived from the Upanishads outlining of differing states of human consciousness, including a fourth state that combines the first three states. Nidra is a practice of the 4th state of consciousness, called yogic sleep.

Regular practice of Nidra has been shown to counter the effects of stress, reduce anxiety, normalize irregular sleep patterns, improve cognition, boost creativity and memory, and promote a renewed sense of self, a coming home. A practice of Nidra may impact the Nervous System similar to 3 hours of sleep.

Nidra scripts are read aloud like guided meditations, and many are available online. Most scripts include the steps below which systematically rotate through koshic layers of being in a subconscious (awake) state.

1. set-up
2. turning inward
3. sankalpa (heart's highest intention)
4. body scan (rotating consciousness)
5. breath awareness (connecting mind and body)
6. opposite sensations or emotions (stimulating homeostasis)
7. visualization (initiating sensations of lightness)
8. reaffirm sankalpa
9. coming back/return to breath and body

Some important notes for Nidra:
- ✓ Scripts may be modified; however, certain steps are needed for rotations of consciousness.
- ✓ As with all yogic practices, practice Yoga Nidra before teaching, or your words may not land.
- ✓ Limiting movements as much as possible supports a beneficial Nidra.
- ✓ There are hundreds of Nidra scripts, this section provided only one sample.
- ✓ Props are recommended for comfort, adjust reclining position for third trimester of pregnancy.

100. Shavayatra Nidra

Set Up, 5 minutes.

Welcome to your practice of Nidra. Gather props to position yourself so that you feel supported.
Enjoy the process of becoming cozy. Arrange your arms comfortably alongside the body, palms facing up.
Make any micro-adjustments now so you feel comfortable in a sort of stillness for this practice.

Turning Inward and Sankalpa, 5-7 minutes.

Feel supported by the surface your body is resting upon, your eyes can remain open or closed.
You will be guided to witness aspects of your mind and body. Whatever you experience is perfect, just as it is.
As you settle into stillness, notice your mind is spontaneously drawn into the present moment.
Witness that there are parts of your body and mind that are instantly able to relax and let go.
Witness that there are other places that still hold on, where there's some kind of resistance.
Perhaps they may not know how to let go. Let there be no sense of struggle. Simply notice.
Be present to all the sensations that are arising in this moment without judgment.
Let go of struggle and be present and generous with yourself in effortlessness, relax all trying.
Bring attention to your senses. Notice the taste in your mouth, the colors behind your eyelids.
Witness the touch of the air on your skin, the sounds around you. Witness that you are alive.
Nothing to do but simply to notice your body breathing.
Breathe in, soaking in freshness and renewal. Breathe out, releasing, unburdened and free.
Set your attention now that you will remain aware throughout the practice.
Allow your heart's deepest desire to arise, a desire for yourself, for another, or for the world.
Whatever it is, welcome and affirm this desire in the present tense as if it's true right now.
Allow your heart to make a statement of profound healing truth.

Body Scan, 10 minutes.

Now bring your attention to your face and allow all expression to relax.
Allow the eyeballs to rest back in their sockets.
Allow the tongue to rest in the mouth as the lower jaw releases, gently opening
Allow the skin on the cheeks and neck to soften towards the floor.
Come aware of the sensations in the tongue, jaw, gums, teeth, lips, the entire mouth.
The cheeks and cheekbones, chin, the earlobes, the inner ear canals, and the outer ears.
Nose, tip of the nose, both nostrils, both eyeballs, the space beneath the eyeballs, both eyelids.
Both eyebrows and the space between the eyebrows.
The temples, forehead, top of head, back of skull, back of neck, the whole face, head, and neck.
Allow sensation to flow to the collarbones, the right shoulder, left shoulder, and down the arms.
To the right wrist, the palm, fingers, the thumb, warm and tingling with presence.
To the left wrist, the palm, fingers, the thumb, warm and tingling with presence.
Simply aware of sensations through the arms, the hands, through the palms, into the fingers.
Now allow your focus to broaden, moving down the torso into the pubic bone in the front.
The sacrum and tailbone in the back.
The entire torso, shoulders, arms, and hands are bathed in an evenly hovering awareness.
Draw attention to this surrounding spaciousness and be this space.
Release attention down into the bowl of the pelvis, sense the energy in the pelvis.
Behind the pubic bone in front and in front of the sacrum in back.
Allow your awareness to spill over into the front of the hip creases.
The right buttock, the left buttock, the groin, everywhere in and around the pelvic girdle.
Awareness fills the thighs, knees, the space under the kneecaps, the hollow in back of the knees.
The right shin, the ankles, the feet, alive with presence. The left shin, the ankles, the feet, alive with presence.
Tingling at the tip of big toes, at the tip of second toes, third toes, fourth toes, little toes.
A soft blanket of attention covering the feet, the ankles, and shins, the thighs, and hips.
The entire torso, belly, chest, back, hands and arms, the shoulders, the neck, the face, and head.
Every cell felt equally in even awareness. Nothing separate. Everything included.

Breath Awareness: Ascending breathing/Shitali karana, 10 minutes.
Repeat exhales down and inhales up each body part pair 3 times each.
Exhale from the top of the head to the toes (inhale from the toes to the top of head).
Exhale from the top of the head to the ankles (inhale back up from ankles to top of head).
Exhale from top of the head to knees (inhale back up from knees to top of head).
Exhale from top of head to perineum at base of spine (inhale up from perineum to head).
Exhale from the top of the head to the navel center (inhale back up from navel to head).
Exhale from the top of the head to the heart center (inhale back up from heart to head).
Exhale from the top of head to the throat (inhale back up from throat to top of head).
Exhale from the top of the head to the bridge between the nostrils (inhale in reverse).
Exhale from the top of the head to the throat (inhale up from the throat to the top of the head)
Exhale down from the top of head to the heart center (inhale back up from heart to head)
Exhale down from top of the head to the navel center (inhale back up from navel to head)
Exhale from top of head to perineum at base of spine (inhale up from perineum to head)
Exhale from the top of the head to the knees (inhale back up from knees to head)
Exhale from the top of the head to the ankles (inhale back up from ankles to top of head)
Exhale from top of head down to toes (inhale from the toes up to the top of the head)

Opposite Sensations, 10 minutes.

Bring attention to feelings of warm or coolness, heavy or lightness, comfort or discomfort, moistness, or dryness.
Welcome both opposite feelings at the same time to experience how doing this affects you.
Now bring attention to an emotion that is present or one that you are working with in your life.
Welcome and invite this emotion with its thoughts, images, or memories that co-arise.
Consider a memory that brings the opposite emotion into your body. Where do you experience this opposite?
Move back and forth between emotions. Experience one, then the other, how each is experienced in the body.
Now, inviting both emotions at the same time, experiencing how this affects your entire body and the mind.
Feeling yourself as the one aware of everything now present, the field of awareness in which everything is arising.

Visualization and Reaffirmation of Sankalpa, 5 minutes.

Now witness sensations throughout your body of happiness or well-being.
A sensation of wonder you might notice in a field of wildflowers with a stream of crystal-clear water nearby.
Perhaps you sense the smell, sounds of wind and water, feel warm rays of the sun.
Recall a memory from your life that invites these feelings of pleasure, joy, or wellbeing into your body.
Perhaps experiencing the sensation of joy as an inner smile that radiates from your heart.
The heart smiling, and this smile expanding through your torso, arms, hands, pelvis, legs, feet.
Flowing up into the head and face, the mouth, lips, and eyes smiling.
The entire body smiling, radiant with the feeling well-being, or being OK just as you are.
Open and spacious awareness in which everything is welcome just as it is.
Sensations, emotions, beliefs, joy, well-being, the experience of being pure awareness.
Now allow your heart's deepest desire to arise again as if it's true right now.
Visualize every cell of your body brightening from your heart's profound healing truth.

Coming Back, 5 minutes.

Now, taking your time transitioning to your alert and wide-awake state of wakefulness.
Sensing your body, the room around you, eyes opening as you feel ready.
Perhaps wiggling your fingers and toes, moving your body, reorienting to where you are.
Eventually rolling onto your right side, curling up into a fetal position… keep the eyes closed.
Experience the feeling of gratitude for taking time to practice welcoming yourself.
Experiencing yourself as timeless, open, and spacious well-being is perfect.
Yourself as unchanging spacious awareness in which everything is unfolding.
Yourself as the embodiment of unfolding this life with the abundance of your heart's desires.
When ready press yourself up into a seated position and bring your hands to your heart.
May this practice bring us peace & may we share that peace with others.

Practice

1. Take a class labeled as Yoga Nidra. Before and after class, note sensations in your body.

   Before: My heart feels ___________, my head feels __________, my feet feel ____________.

   After: My heart feels ___________, my head feels __________, my feet feel ____________.

Qigong

Surrender your fall into a world that is not concrete.
Hard does not equal real.

Qigong's origins go back thousands of years in China, where it remains an essential part of Traditional Chinese Medicine (TCM) and is the foundation of Tai Chi. Qigong practices are adaptable to any person or situation and can decrease symptoms of stress, fatigue, and pain, while also improving balance, organ health, circulation, flexibility, strength, immunity, clarity, energy, optimism, and joy.

Qigong utilizes Yin and Yang concepts as well as meridians, and energy centers called Dantians. The lower Dantian is Jing, the seat of strength), the middle is Qi, the energy of life, and the upper Dantian is Shen, spirit, and higher consciousness. Qigong impacts all subtle energies (Doshas, Chakras, Vayus, etc.) as Qigong movements are similar to directions of energy in nature.

Though at first Qigong can feel awkward, fusing Qigong into yoga practice can cultivate great harmony within that then transfers to one's experience of life. To fuse Qigong into a Hatha practice, try add movements at Mountain, as a warm-up to other practice, as preparation for savasana, or as added energetic elements to Squat, Goddess, Low and Crescent Lunges; however, Qigong can be and is a practice in and of itself for a lifetime. Some important notes for Qigong are:

- ✓ There are thousands of Qigong movements, though naming conventions can be confusing.
- ✓ Many Qigong practices in this section are combined to experience complimentary movements; however, they can be performed by themselves or in almost any sequence.
- ✓ Qigong allows differing methodologies and individual experience of what feels most harmonic.
- ✓ While most Qigong movements provided here are cued as standing postures, wherever needed, one can do most movements from a chair or reclining with great benefit.
- ✓ Though no cautions are listed for these movements, people with vertigo and certain heart conditions may find that slowing movements down and decreasing angles will allow greater ease; however, this is not a substitute for medical advice.

101. Knocking on the Door of Life and Laughter

Cues. Natural breathing, or open mouth exhales.

Feet wider than shoulder width, knees, and shoulders soft and relaxed.

Alternate one arm in front of torso and other behind torso,

swing arms side to side.

Neck and torso alternate left and right to follow arm in front.

When warmed up, arms swings turn into body taps (open or closed hands).

Tap body at pelvis level, at kidney level, and at lung level or shoulder level.

Suggested movement time is 3-5 minutes.

To finish, allow uncontrolled laughter for at least 1 minute.

102. Qi Tapping

Cues. Natural breathing and stance of feet shoulder width or wider.

Choose soft fists, open palms, or fingers for tapping

(force enough to wake up tissue, but not to hurt).

Rub hands for heat, rub fingernails.

Tap backs of hands together, then sternum.

Tap jaw, temples, 3rd eye, top of head, back of neck, shoulders, lungs.

Open one arm (thumb points out) to tap down inside of arm to palm,

flip palm to tap up arm.

Tap back over to lungs, move to other arm and repeat.

Tap down sides of abdomen, tap up and down sides of lumbar spine.

Tap down backs (or sides) of legs to ankles, tap up front (or inside) of legs.

Suggested movement time is 3-5 minutes.

103. Shaking, Arm/Heel Drops and Qi Sway

Cues. Natural breathing, shaking sounds, sighs, and open mouth exhales.

Feet at shoulder width, use enough force to stimulate joints and spine.

Raise one arm to side and drop hand to body, repeat on other side,

then lift and drop both at once.

Raise feet by lifting heels, then drop heels.

Raise and drop arms/heels at the same time and repeat a few times.

Bounce/shake, rotate wrists, bend elbows to raise/lower hands.

Lift foot, shake and swing it, rotate it in circles, repeat other foot.

Bounce whole body, arms and legs can swing and rotate in circles.

To finish, narrow stance so feet touch,

bring hands above head like a compass needle, let body sway.

Suggested movement time is 3-5 minutes.

104. Side Bend Figure 8 and Heaven and Earth

Cues.
Feet wider than shoulder width, knees, and shoulders soft and relaxed.

Place left hand (open) on left side of hip/leg, right palm on right side.

Bend torso to side, hand slides down leg, hand on other side slides up,

repeat both sides several times.

Add lifting heel and turning head on side that hand rises.

Create a figure 8 motion between sides, repeat figure 8 several times.

For Heaven and Earth, bring palms to face in front of chest.

Extend right hand with palm up upward to right,

press left hand with palm down downward on left side.

Hands alternate up/down, palms face at chest between, repeat.

To finish, place hands near heart, one on top of the other,

notice vibration in heart.

Suggested movement time is 3-5 minutes.

105. Swimming Dragon

Cues.
Natural breathing, feet at shoulder width, knees, and shoulders soft.

Movement is fluid and methodical, but dragon can dive and play.

Create dragon, place palms, base of hands/fingers together, fingers up.

Bend elbows/knees, lean and rotate right as dragon swims toward right side.

Bend wrists, turn hands toward left and repeat as dragon moves to left side.

Swim dragon across front torso, repeating wrist, and knee bends,

and neck and torso rotation as dragon alternates sides and repeats laps.

To finish, dragon swims and rises overhead, gaze upward.

Place hands on abdomen in upside-down triangle shape, notice sensations.

Suggested movement time is 3-5 minutes.

106. Circle the Sun

Cues.
Natural breathing, feet wider than shoulder width.

Knees and shoulders soft and relaxed.

Shoulders, elbows, and wrist joints are fluid.

Hands move slowly and feel air when moving.

Hands in front of pelvis, palms face, without touching.

Rotate body slightly to the right,

inhale arms upward like a half circle towards front.

Exhale to left side to complete circle, hands return to sides of hips.

Repeat movement several times.

To finish, place hands on abdomen, notice sensations.

Suggested movement time is 5 minutes.

107. Spinal Cord Breathing and Spreading Feathers

Cues.   Natural breathing, feet shoulder width, knees and shoulders soft and relaxed.

Movements are in spine and arms, do not hinge forward from waist.

Inhale cactus arms, elbows into side ribs, lift chest, open throat, spine arches.

Exhale forearms touch at chest as chin/tailbone tuck inward, spine rounds.

Repeat forward and back Spinal Cord breathing several times.

Rotate torso to sides during cactus arms, return to center as forearms touch.

Return to neutral spine for Spreading Feathers.

Inhale arms to sides, elbows slightly bent, thumbs face up.

Exhale lower arms, turn thumbs down, pinkies face up.

Alternate lowering ear/tilting chin right or left when hands low.

Repeat Spreading Feathers several times.

Then place hands on abdomen, notice sensations.

Suggested movement time is 5 minutes.

108. Painting, Wild Geese, and Parting Clouds

Cues.   Natural breathing, feet wider than shoulder width, knees, and shoulders soft and relaxed.

Shoulders, elbows, and wrist joints are fluid, hands move slowly through air.

Hands in front, inhale arms up to face level, flex wrist joints, fingers up.

Exhale hands down to start point, wrist joints extend, fingers down.

Repeat several times, return to center, and extend hands to opposite sides.

Gaze to right as right arm raises with wrist hinged like wing, lower right hand.

Gaze shifts to left and left arm raises as left wrist hinges.

Alternate weight by coming on toes of foot on side of raised arm.

Repeat Geese several times, return to center, cross wrists at pelvis level.

For Clouds, inhale arms up in circle to above head, palms face forward.

Exhale hands to start point in circular motion.

Repeat Parting Clouds several times.

Place hands on heart, notice sensations.

Suggested movement time is 5 minutes.

109. 6 Healing Sounds

Cues.   Inhale through the nose, exhale sounds. Suggested movement time is 5 minutes.

a.   Raise hands, palms face up, look up. Inhale white light, like a beautiful cloud. Exhale 'sssssss' as hands are placed over lungs, courage over grief.

b.   Kidneys. Hands on knees with back rounded. Inhale blue light like sunlight on water. Exhale 'choooo' as hands are placed over kidneys, peace over fear.

c.   Liver. Raise hands, interlock fingers, look up and lean left. Inhale green light, a sunny forest. Exhale 'shhhhh' as hands go to liver, kindness over anger.

d.   Heart. Raise hands, interlock fingers, look up, lean right. Inhale red light, a low fire. Exhale 'haaaaa' as hands are placed on heart, love over hate.

e.   Spleen. Press hands on left side of rib cage. Inhale yellow light like the sun's vitality. Exhale 'whoooo' with hands over spleen, trust over worry.

f.   Triple warmer. 'Heeeee' sound as hands float up/down dantians, harmony over stress. To Finish. Both hands make circles around lower abdomen like rainbows, harmony.

110. Chi Ball

Cues.   Natural breathing, feet wider than shoulder width, knees, and shoulders soft and relaxed.

Rub hands, then hold hands (palms face) about 6" apart in front of abdomen.

Notice energy between hands, use that energy as a ball.

Pulse hands in and out at ball edges several times, playing with the ball size.

Pulse one hand further away so energy grows between hands like a wave.

Then shape energy ball again.

Do this in both directions several times.

Next use hand movements to rotate the ball on its axis,

and to fan the energy's flame.

Finally, make the ball smaller by pulsing palms a few inches apart.

When energy is concentrated, place stacked hands on lower abdomen.

Warm with energy you transformed.

Suggested movement time is 5 minutes.

Indigenous Practices

Deep in footsteps walked by ancestors in toils, triumphs, angst and in joy.
Is this path I trod now enough for me to grow, for them, for all?
I feel it, the cells of all that has been and that will be.
Oh, but the beauty of seeing it now clinging to my soul.
In this moment I know what I have always known.
I am the embodied fruits of their labors,
And we shall bloom into love abiding here and now,
so generations to come feel at home with what has been planted here.

Indigenous refers to people that are native to, or have ancestral history with, a geographical area prior to colonization, forced migration or other form of subjugation. Wisdom tradition practices are one way to learn about and honor wellness rituals that can improve connections with ourselves and with all people collectively.

Sacred ritual practices are performed in many cultures and typically include similarities of genuine internal motivation, meaningful symbolism, storytelling, a sense of belonging, and the performance of tasks. In addition to the practices provided here, there are many other Indigenous wisdom practices and rituals involving music, dance, prayer, celebration of seasons and life events occurring in all indigenous cultures, as well colonial ones. Some important notes for Indigenous Practices are:

- ✓ It is best to experience these practices through those with lived experience and ancestral teachings. If you do not have access to such teachers, you can begin with some basic practices at home.
- ✓ Avoid promoting incorrect assumptions when blending practices. For example, if combining the 4 Directions with Qigong Knocking on the Door of Life, name the separate practices and origins so they don't show up as some formulation of New Age Spirituality – which they are not.

111. 4 Directions

Meaning. Honoring the elements of life.

Benefits. Promotes gratitude, awareness, and connection.

Origins. Sacred rituals ofe 4 directions are in most indigenous traditions.

Basics below are adapted from practices of N. American tribes.

The picture provided is a medicine wheel symbol.

Basics. Stand and face each direction and repeat mentally or out loud.

The East, sun rise, beginnings, opportunity to begin again.

The South, fullness of day, creativity, honoring the playfulness of youth.

The West, sun sets when day is done, time for introspection and reflection.

The North, darkness, connection with our ancestors, patience, compassion, silence.

The Center, a rainbow of the present moment, timeless grace.

Ritualize. In the morning or evening as gratitude, or any time for an elevated sense of connection.

Add smudging with sage, cedar, pine, or palo santo to cleanse the space you are in.

112. Smudging

Meaning. To cleanse or neutralize air in a space, person, or item.

Benefits. Can freshen and cleanse air to support respiratory health.

Can repel insects and remove negativity and stress.

Origins. Smudging is a sacred ritual of mostly N. American indigenous peoples, who were banned from it for years as colonizers labeled it sacrilegious.

Palo santo is used for similar purposes in S. America.

Commercializing sage can harm indigenous peoples who depend upon sustained availability of ritual white sage.

Source sage responsibly and leave the plant's root so it can grow.

The basics below include a traditional N. American Cherokee prayer.

Basics. Prepare a sage bundle, fireproof container, and feather.

Light the end of the sage so it smolders and smokes (do not allow flames).

Hold the bundle and direct smoke with feather (or fan with your hand).

When needed, use your container to collect the ash.

Fan smoke to areas of body below and repeat mentally or out loud.

May your hands be cleansed, that they create beautiful things.

May your feet be cleansed, that they may take you where you most need to be.

May your heart be cleansed, that you might hear its messages clearly.

May your throat be cleansed, so that you might speak rightly when words are needed.

May your eyes be cleansed, so that you might see the signs and wonders of the world.

Ritualize. In personal or group meditation, using sage, copal, myrrh, frankincense, or juniper.

Follow sage with sweetgrass.

Use caution to avoid unwanted fire.

113. Prayer Flags

Meaning. Sending goodwill intentions into the world.

Benefits. Can promote expression, connection to others/lineage.

Origins. Many cultures have used prayer flags for thousands of years, such as in India, Nepal, China and in North, Central and South America, and other cultures around the world.

Specifics of prayer flags depend upon the culture or origin.

Cues. Gather ethically sourced naturally colored cloth to prepare.

Many indigenous N. American tribes recognize colors (red, yellow, black, white) relating to life's natural and spiritual elements. Tibetan Buddhists recognize 5 elemental colors for harmony (blue/space, white/air, red/fire, blue/space, green/water, yellow/earth).

Chakra flags represent the elemental colors of chakras, primarily from Tantric traditions.

To send a message or intention, rip off a cloth strip in your color choice.

Then tie the cloth so it can be fastened to a branch or other item outdoors.

Your intention then belongs to the air, which will carry it where it needs to go.

Hearing messages in the wind is not an auditory process, but an electromagnetic force.

Preparing a prayer flag can be a gift to yourself and to others.

Ritualize. In personal or group ceremony to invite global awareness and connection.

Ensure location for placing flags allows such items.

114. Ritual Cacao

Cautions. Contains small amounts of caffeine.

Meaning. Conduit between ancient wisdom and the inner self.

Benefits. Cacao is a superfood due to its nutritional anti-oxidants.

It is also known as a heart-opener due to its production of beta-endorphins in the brain for relaxation and happiness.

It can also increase circulation and reduce inflammation.

Origins. A Mayan/Mesoamerican practice in sacred ceremonies to bridge physical and spiritual worlds. Ceremonial cacao differs from other products made from Theobroma cacao tree (such as cocoa and chocolate) and thus retains the nutritional qualities of the raw bean.

Basics. The basics here relate to current and frequent indigenous ceremonial cacao use by Mayans in Guatemala where ceremonial cacao is single ingredient, sustainably sourced, minimally processed and traditionally made with loving intentions into a block of cacao.

To feel the benefits of ceremonial cacao as a conduit of ancient wisdom and the inner self, one must fuse sincere intention into the final preparation of ceremonial cacao.

- ✓ Cut some shavings from your block of ceremonial cacao.
- ✓ Add from 1 tsp to 1 TBSP of cacao shaving to water and heat.
- ✓ Add cinnamon, cardamom, and cayenne pepper to taste.

Sip with mindfulness of cacao properties, those who made it possible, and heart intention.

Ritualize. From preparation until last sip, enjoy a sacred meditation and commune with self.

Sip cacao infused with mantra, meditation, or heartfelt conversations into the ceremony.

115. Holi Celebration (Holi = Burning; also called Festival of Colors)

Cautions. Use natural powders that are non-toxic and safe for eyes, mouth, and skin.

Meaning. Represents return to light over darkness, abundance over stagnation.

Benefits. Provokes playfulness, joy, connection, and positive change.

Origins. Archeologists date the first inscription of Holi as 300 BCE in India. Some traditions cite a love story - Krishna wanted to attract Radha and so played a game with her using colored powder. Other stories cite Prahalad, a son who wanted to worship against his father's wishes. Prahalad's sister Holika tried to burn him, but ended up burning herself instead, so her ashes represented transformation. Holi is traditionally on the last full moon in March, marking the end of winter.

Basics. One of many ways to perform color throwing:
Gather non-toxic, naturally dyed powders in bowls, water, and coconut oil (for skin).
Gather people, inform them to wear natural fibers that will take on colors best.
Present the stories of Holi and allow time for playfulness representing the stories.
Apply coconut oil if desired to skin to make colors stick to skin more vibrantly.
Start with partners applying colors to one another's faces.
After faces are complete, gather in a circle and start throwing colors.

Ritualize. Try another Holi ritual of throwing cow dung into a fire while shouting obscenities to represent cleansing. Or invoke a spring cleaning at home and burn that which can't be cleaned (make sure items are safe to burn) with an intention of releasing stagnate energy.

116. Mandala (Mandala = Circle)

Meaning. Spiritual guidance tool.

Benefits. Increases 3rd eye balance, mental focus, supports inner guidance, promotes creativity and can support deep sleep/dream recall.

Origins. Found in written text and in an image in the Rig Veda, but similar representations have been found in most civilizations, and are still used daily in Taoist, Yoga, Ayurveda, and Mayan offerings.
The mandala can represent a vision board of what you are drawn to, a map of devotion, the entire universe, a connection from the inner self to the spiritual world, and more.

Basics. For an indoors mandala, gather material without planning what you will create.
Gather items like paper, canvas, pencils, pens, markers, paints, cloth, thread, beads, etc.
For a nature mandala, gather items natural to area such as flowers, rocks, seashells, pinecones, plants, etc. (do this with minimal environmental disruption).
Start your mandala by forming a circle and dividing that circle into four equal quadrants.
Place something in one quadrant and repeat it in the same location in the other quadrants.
Then add the next thing and repeat, so step by step, mandalas form into a journey.

Ritualize. After preparing your circle and quadrants, add a few items at night and in the morning.
Allow additions to come naturally, without thought.

117. **Mala making** (Mala = Garland)

Meaning.   Prayer beads to focus intention.

Benefits.   Overall benefits include elevated self-awareness, focus and mindfulness. Additional benefits vary based on materials used.

Origins.   Ancient yogic sages utilized malas, and stories of the Buddha also cite their prevalence. Beads strung together for prayer are also found in Islam and Christianity. The number of 108 is derived from Vedic cosmology. 108 represents universal consciousness (determined by ancient mathematicians as the ratio and distance of the sun to earth and similar calculations). Malas typically consist of 108 beads plus a guru bead to mark the beginning and end.

Basics.   Consider your intention for the mala.

Is there a quality that you desire more of such as material stability or spiritual connection? Your intention guides your material selections.

Most malas include 108 beads, or some derivative of less beads (such as 54 or 21).

- ✓ Gather your materials (natural beads made from wood, seeds, or gemstones in 6,8 or 10mm sizes, a guru bead, embroidery thread for the tassel, cord, wire, and scissors).
- ✓ Choose a mantra or affirmation you'll use when creating your mala.
- ✓ As you place each bead on the cord, repeat your mantra.
- ✓ When all beads are on your cord, stretch the cord before tying the ends together.
- ✓ Create tassel by wrapping thread around all fingers at same time for 12-18 repetitions.
- ✓ Tie your tassel near one end before cutting open the other end.
- ✓ Use wire to thread tassel end through a guru bead and affix tassel ring over the knot.

Ritualize.   Use to chant mantra repetitions, as an intention reminder, or to count 108 sun salutations.

Practice

1.   Share Sacred Wisdom in Ritual

    Review Indigenous Practices. Choose two practices to share with at least 1 other person.
Before and after each practice, name sensations in your body.

>   Before: My heart feels ____________, my head feels __________, my feet feel ____________.
>   After: My heart feels ___________, my head feels __________, my feet feel ___________.

2.   Mantra

    Chant or sing the Bliss Mantra or another affirmation that elevates your awareness of spiritual self and connection to others in the essence of their spirit. Try this for at least 3 minutes.

I am the light of my soul.
I am beautiful.
I am bountiful.
I am bliss.
I am.

Chapter 4

Subtle Techniques

We are far more complex than our physical matter alone.

Subtle energy is not visible by physical imaging, but the power of it is so vast that it is felt in all we do. It adds human experiential dimension to our physical form and is is explained in various languages by differing traditions. For all of yoga's history, ancient yogis seemed to understand the importance of energy movement in wellness. Early yogic views focused on the nature of energy, including the most subtle of energetic forces, to ascertain how to move energy consciously for wellness.

Energy In = Energy Out

Though much emphasis in modern yoga is placed upon physical poses, just doing poses can mean one misses out on many more subtle energy benefits. For example, if someone performs a sequence of poses without consciously breathing with those poses, positive impact can be limited to the musculoskeletal system, rather than also promoting shifts in energy, mood, and to positive perspectives.

Other subtle energy practices of Hatha yoga practice can be fused with poses to access more dynamic benefits for your mind and body. Most techniques in this book outline subtle energy impacts or techniques, so that everyone can perpetuate additional benefits in their practice and sequences.

Subtle energy practice techniques in this chapter include:

Pranayama (breathing techniques)

Energetic Aids (drishtis, bandhas, mudras)

Mantra (mind focus)

Meditation (state of being/doing nothing)

Hatha yoga practice benefits can also be increased through the understanding of vayus, chakras and doshas that can support practice sequencing choices. Subtle energy considerations included here are:

Vayu practices (*energy directions*)

Chakra practices (*energy centers*)

Dosha practices (*physical constitution in harmony*)

Important general notes for Subtle Energy practices are:
- ✓ Subtle Energy practices provided are not meant to be sequenced in order.
- ✓ Cautions presented cannot cover all variables and are not a substitute for medical advice.
- ✓ Sequence ideas for each practice under are a sample of possibilities.

Pranayama (Breathing)

If the mind wants to reach for something, give it a breath.

Prana, the breath, means life force in Sanskrit, and everything that breathes has prana. Breathing techniques in yoga are called the practice of pranayama in (Sanskrit for the regulation of breath). Changes to breathing impact all human functions, and evidence of the benefits of breath regulation are widely documented.

In general, nose breathing warms air for ease in bodily operations and it stimulates the vagus nerve to benefit the nervous system. Mouth breathing is less useful for the body but can surface emotions. Isolating sides breath to one side of the nostril impacts either the sympathetic or parasympathetic system. Slower breathing patterns and longer exhales are calming, and fast breaths or longer inhales are energizing. Incorporating the tongue into breath can cool temperature and increase immunity.

This Pranayam section includes categories of breathing techniques, but not all will work similarly for all people. The categories included are based upon general effect for most people, and they are:

> Balancing
> Cooling/Soothing
> Warming/Energizing
> Emotional Release

Some important notes for Pranayama are:

- ✓ Prior to beginning breathing techniques, first take a few conscious inhales and exhales.
- ✓ There are many more yogic breathing techniques than those included in this section.
- ✓ Suggested times for all breathing techniques are from 1 to 11 minutes.
- ✓ Cautions related to breathing techniques should not be taken lightly.
- ✓ Cautions presented cannot cover all variables and are not a substitute for medical advice.

Balancing Breaths

118. **Durga** (3-part breath)

Chakras/Doshas/Vayus. Sacral, Solar Plexus, Heart/All/Inward, balancing.
Cautions. None.
Benefits. Promotes a sense of calm, focus, and present awareness.
Cues. Inhale 3 counts

1st count inhale to expand lower abdomen.

2nd count inhale to fill center of torso.

3rd count inhale to expand chest.

Exhale in reverse.

Complete several full rounds of 3 parts in and 3 parts out.
Sequence. For present moment awareness and mind-body connection.
Variations. Place hands at each location to feel the breath moving through each position.

119. **Sama Vritti** (Sama = Equal, Vritti = Breath; also called Box Breathing)

Chakras/Doshas/Vayus. Sacral, Solar Plexus, Heart/All/Inward, balancing.
Cautions. Pre-natal and heart conditions.
Benefits. Promotes nervous system balance, clarity, and calm presence.
Cues. Focus breath in abdomen and torso as in Durga breath.

Inhale through nose for 4 counts, suspend inhale 4 counts.

Exhale through nose for 4 counts, suspend exhale 4 counts.

Complete several full rounds of 4/4/4/4.
Sequence. For present moment awareness and mind-body connection.
Variations. Increase or decrease counts.

Inhale 4 counts up left side torso.

Suspend in 4 counts across chest to right side of torso.

Exhale 4 counts down right side.

Suspend out 4 counts across low abdomen to left side of torso.

120. **Ujjayi** (Ujjayi = Victorious; also called Ocean breath)

Chakras/Doshas/Vayus. Solar Plexus, Throat/All/Inward, downward, balancing, expanding.
Cautions. Pre-natal, eye, respiratory or heart conditions.
Benefits. Stimulates vagus nerve, metabolism, and body heat.

Can both uplift and ground energy.
Cues. Breathe through nose with slight constriction in back of throat.

Breath is audible like an ocean wave as it vibrates over vocal cords.

Inhales and exhales are long and equal.
Sequence. During vinyasa and when desiring increased internal heat.
Variations. Equal count breath with slight constriction in back of throat.

121. Channel Clearing Breath - Nadi Shodhana (Nadi = channel, shodhana = cleaning, purifying)

Chakras/Doshas/Vayus. All/All/ Inward, downward, balancing, upward.

Cautions.　　Pre-natal, seizure disorders, low blood pressure, dizziness, and headache conditions.

Benefits.　　Supports nervous system and respiratory balance, clarity, alertness, and concentration.

Cues.　　Breaths are silent, slow, and equal with slight suspension on inhales and exhales.

Place index/middle fingers on bridge of nose.

Thumb closes a nostril; ring finger closes other.

Close right nostril, inhale through left nostril.

Close left nostril and suspend breath briefly.

Open right nostril, exhale right side and suspend breath briefly.

Inhale right nostril then close right and suspend breath briefly.

Open left nostril, exhale left side and suspend breath briefly.

Inhale left nostril to begin 2nd round.

Start with 5 rounds, end with left nostril exhale.

Sequence.　　Before savasana or meditation.

Variations.　　Try left and/or right nostril breathing instead.

Cooling/Soothing Breaths

122. Segmented Breath for Soothing

Chakras/Doshas/Vayus. Root/All except excess Kapha/Inward, downward.

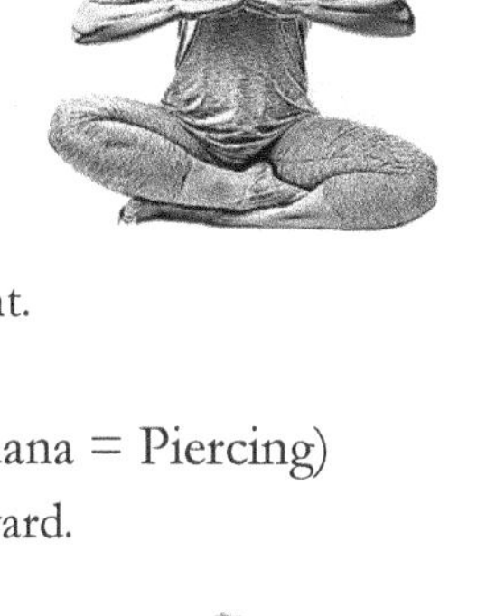

Cautions.   Low blood pressure and poor circulation.
Benefits.   Can reduce tension, increase clarity, and promote relaxation.
Cues.   Nostrils are relaxed; motion is felt in the diaphragm.
                  Each breath part is equal and divided by a slight suspension.
                  Inhale for 4 parts, each segment rising through torso
                  Exhale 8 parts out back to beginning point.
Sequence.   To downregulate energy.
Variations.   Decrease length of exhale to practice building up to full 8 count.

123. Left Nostril Breath - Chandra Bhedana (Chandra = Moon; Bhedana = Piercing)

Chakras/Doshas/Vayus. Root/All except excess Kapha/Inward, downward.

Cautions.   Low blood pressure and poor circulation.
Benefits.   Can improve sleep, cool body, and reduce tension.
Cues.   Lightly block right nostril with thumb or finger, inhale left nostril.
                  Lightly block left nostril with thumb or finger, exhale right nostril.
                  Continue inhaling through left nostril and exhaling through right.
                  Inhales and exhales are long and equal.
                  Repeat several rounds, working up to 5 minutes at one time.
Sequence.   To prepare for rest and for cooling and calming down.
Variations.   Breathe only through left nostril (both inhale and exhale).

124. Hissing Breath – Sheetkari (Sheetkari = Cooling)

Chakras/Doshas/Vayus. Root, Throat/All except excess Kapha/Inward, downward.

Cautions.   Low blood pressure and poor circulation.
Benefits.   Can improve sleep, cool body, and reduce tension and thirst.
Cues.   Roll tongue to place bottom of tongue on roof of mouth.
                  Press upper and lower jaw together, open lips to bare teeth.
                  Inhale through open mouth in a hissing sound, suspend breath.
                  Close lips and exhale through nose.
Sequence.   To prepare for rest and to let go of steam.
Variations.   Thumb on nail of pinky finger and other fingers.

125. **Sipping Breath - Sitali** (Sitali = Cooling)

Chakras/Doshas/Vayus. Root, Throat/All except excess Kapha/Inward, downward.

Cautions.	Low blood pressure and poor circulation.
Benefits.	Can improve sleep, cool body, and reduce tension and thirst.
Cues.	Lower chin, curl tongue lengthwise and push it out of mouth.
	Inhale through "straw" made by curled tongue as chin lifts up.
	Exhale through nose (close mouth) as chin lowers/tong retracts.
Sequence.	Preparing for rest and when desiring a cooling and calming down.
Variations.	Perform Sheetkari if unable to curl tongue.

126. **Whistle Breath** (Also called Beak Breath)

Chakras/Doshas/Vayus. Root, Throat/All/Inward, downward, balancing.

Cautions.	Low blood pressure.
Benefits.	Stimulates vagus nerve and thyroid, promotes calm inner tranquility.
Cues.	Pucker lips to inhale, making a whistle noise. Exhale through nose.
Sequence.	To focus on inner calm.
Variations.	Inhale through nose and exhale through puckered lips.

127. **Humming Breath - Bhramari** (Bhramari = Big Black Bee)

Chakras/Doshas/Vayus. Depends on tone/All/Inward, upward, downward.

Cautions.	Low blood pressure.
Benefits.	Stimulates digestion and promotes sense of contentment.
Cues.	Place thumbs on external parts of ear canal to reduce noise.
	Inhale through nose, exhale (mouth closed) in a humming sound.
	Experiment with differing tones to adjust frequency.
Sequence.	Preparation for meditation and to calm energy in a group.
Variations.	Fold earlobes over with thumbs.
	Place index fingers over eyes, middle fingers on nostrils,
	ring fingers above top lip and pinky fingers below bottom lip.

128. **Caliber of Life**

Chakras/Doshas/Vayus. Root, Heart, 3rd Eye/All except excess Kapha/Inward, downward.

Cautions.	Dizziness and low blood pressure.
Benefits.	Can improve sleep and reduce tension.
	Can strengthen nervous system and arms and shoulders.
Cues.	Bring arms straight out in front (elbows straight).
	Close right hand into fist, wrap left fingers over fist
	Base of palms touch, thumbs up.
	Gaze at thumbs with slight neck lock.
	Inhale 5 seconds, exhale 5 sec, hold breath out for 15 sec.
Sequence.	Before rest and to ease negativity and fear.
Variations.	Rest hands on a surface or perform the breath without mudra.

Warming/Energizing Breaths

129. Breath of Fire - Kapalabhati (Kapalabhati = Skull Shining)

Chakras/Doshas/Vayus. Solar, 3rd Eye/All except excess Pitta/Inward, upward, expanding.

Cautions. Pre-natal, heavy menstruation, heart, eye, nervous system, and balance conditions.

Benefits. Increases circulation, stamina, and focus.
Can boost immune, respiratory, and digestive systems.
Can reduce negative emotions, stress, and addictive impulses.

Cues. To learn, place hand on low abdomen and pant like a dog.
Close mouth, recreate abdominal action breathing through nose.
There is no rigidity of hands, feet, face, or abdomen.
Exhale through nose powerfully, navel toward spine.
Inhale through nose naturally without trying.
Inhales and exhales are rapid (approx. 2-3 rounds per second).
Begin with 1 minute, build up to longer.

Sequence. Before or after eating by 2 hours and to burn off distractions.

Variations. Add brow drishti to relieve light-headedness; or slow breath to 1 round/second to learn.
Bhastrika, or Bellows Breath, is similar except inhales and exhales are forceful.

130. Right Nostril - Surya Bhedana (Surya = Sun; Bhedana = Piercing)

Chakras/Doshas/Vayus. Solar, 3rd Eye/All except excess Pitta/Inward, upward, expanding.

Cautions. Pre-natal, heart, respiratory and eye conditions.

Benefits. Stimulates sympathetic nervous system, increases circulation, energy, clarity.

Cues. Lightly block left nostril with thumb or finger, inhale right nostril.
Lightly block right nostril with thumb or finger, exhale left nostril.
Continue inhaling through right nostril, exhaling through left.
Breath parts are long/equal; repeat several rounds up to 5 min.

Sequence. For increased internal heat for clarity and/or digestion.

Variations. Breathe only through right nostril (both inhale and exhale).

131. Breath of Joy

Chakras/Doshas/Vayus. Solar, Heart, Throat/All except excess Vata/Inward, upward, expanding.

Cautions. Pre-natal, anxiety, vertigo, eye, shoulder, and heart conditions.

Benefits. Increases energy, clarity, focus, and positivity.

Cues. Segment breath into 3 inhales followed by 1 exhale.
Inhale straight arms in front of torso to chest level with palms up.
Inhale straight arms out to sides at shoulder level with palms up.
Inhale straight arms overhead, palms facing.
Hinge at waist and bow (arms behind), exhale open mouth "ha" noise.

Sequence. For uplifted energy or to quickly adjust mood and/or ease tension.

Variations. Inhale arms to sides, then front, then upward, then downward.
Bring arms to neutral between movements.

132. Segmented Breath for Energy

Chakras/Doshas/Vayus. Solar, Heart, Throat/All except excess Vata/Inward, upward.

Cautions.　　Pre-natal, anxiety and heart conditions.

Benefits.　　Increases energy, clarity, focus, and positivity.

Cues.　　Nostrils are relaxed; motion is felt in the diaphragm.

Each breath part is equal and divided by a slight suspension.

Inhale for 4 parts, each segment rising through torso

Exhale 1 part out back to beginning point.

Sequence.　　For uplifted energy and increased focus.

Variations.　　Use 8 parts in and 4 parts out for more focused energy.

Add palms up on inhale segments, palms down on exhales.

Emotional Release Breaths

133. Qigong Heart Sound

Chakras/Doshas/Vayus. Heart, Throat/All/Inward, upward, balancing, expanding.
Cautions. None.
Benefits. Can promote a sense of joy for no reason at all.
Cues. Raise hands overhead, interlock fingers, look up and lean right.
Inhale warm red light like a low fire.
Exhale 'haaaaa' as one or both hands are placed on heart.
Repeat several times.
Sequence. To boost feelings of self-compassion.
Variations. Make the sound "haaaaa" only, without using hands.

134. Lion's Breath - Simhasana (Simba = Lion)

Chakras/Doshas/Vayus. Throat/All/Inward, upward, expanding.
Cautions. Dizziness and low blood pressure.
Benefits. Stimulates thyroid, immune system and confidence.
Can reduce tension and congestion in chest, neck, and throat.
Cues. Eyes wide open gazing slightly upward.
Inhale through nose, exhale loud "haaaa" (tongue out or not)
Roar for a few rounds, build up to 1 minute at a time.
Sequence. To boost immunity and release tension.
Variations. From Table, inhale forward, exhale backward and roar.
From Squat, hands on thighs with palms up, inhale rise with
arms overhead, exhale/roar to squat/hands to thighs.

135. Cannon

Chakras/Doshas/Vayus. Heart, Throat/All except excess Vata/ Inward, upward, expanding.
Cautions. Dizziness and low blood pressure.
Benefits. Stimulates immune, respiratory system and upper digestive tract.
Can calm feelings of anger.
Cues. Eyes closed, mouth open like an "O."
Breathe through open mouth with strong exhales.
Sequence. To boost immunity and to release anger.
Variations. Inhale long slow and deep through nose, suspend,
then exhale big cannon fire.

136. **Tattva Balance** (Tattva = element; also called Kriya to go Beyond Stress and Duality)

Chakras/Doshas/Vayus. Heart, Throat, 3rd Eye/All/Inward, upward, expanding.

Cautions.	Low blood pressure.
Benefits.	Supports immunity, respiratory health.
	Promotes a sense of harmony with nature and internal power.
Cues.	Place hands in Hakini mudra, gaze at tip of nose.
	Inhale, long, slow, and deeply through nose.
	Exhale through mouth in O shape in 8 equal strokes
	(draw navel point in on each).
	Repeat several times, to finish, suspend inhale for 10-30 seconds.
Sequence.	To boost immunity and to feel a sense of homeostasis.
Variations.	Hakini mudra in front of chest or throat as container for firing breath.

137. **Long Deep Breathing, Open Mouth Exhales**

Chakras/Doshas/Vayus. Heart, Throat/All/Inward, downward.

Cautions.	Can release sadness and grief quickly.
	Recommended to follow this with an uplifted breath.
Benefits.	Can ease anxiety, release emotions, and increase awareness.
Cues.	Inhale long and deep through nose.
	Exhale through slightly open mouth without tension.
Sequence.	To bring emotions to the surface and in some Kundalini kriyas.
Variations.	Extend arms in front, right palm up, left palm down,
	elbows and hands around diaphragm level for nervous system balance.

138. **Caliber of Constant Authority**

Chakras/Doshas/Vayus. Heart, Throat, 3rd Eye/All/Inward, downward.

Cautions.	Can release sadness and grief quickly.
Benefits.	Can ease anxiety, release emotions, and increase present awareness.
Cues.	Bring hands into fists, press knuckles together at heart, gaze at nose.
	Inhale through nose fully, exhale from mouth fully with pursed lips.
	Then inhale fully through pursed lips, exhale fully through nose.
Sequence.	To bring emotions to the surface.
Variations.	Gaze downward at heart-shaped hands or perform without mudra.

Drishtis (Gazes)

Where your focus goes, your energy flows.

Many asana cues include where to set your gaze, even when those cues only specify head position. But Drishti (Sanskrit for eyesight or vision), is more than simply turning your head or looking in a certain direction.   Drishtis are intentional gazes with a soft focus toward "everything and nothing at the same time" that can allow distractions to fall away and positive energy flow to increase. One of the greatest challenges in Drishti practice lies is your mind's ability to think about many things at once and/or to attach meaning to what is seen. Some important notes for Drishtis are:

✓ Take breaks when needed to avoid eye strain. Subtle energy is most powerful when it is not forced.

✓ Cautions presented cannot cover all variables and are not a substitute for medical advice.

139. Tip of Nose – Nasagra Drishti (also called 9/10s gaze)

Chakras/Doshas/Vayus. Root, 3rd Eye/All/Inward, downward.

Cautions. Eye conditions.

Benefits. Promotes calmness, introspection, and focus.

Cues. To learn, hold finger in front of eyes, slowly move finger inward as gaze follows. Gaze may result in seeing a "V" at tip of nose.

Sequence. Upward Facing Dog and Caliber for Constant Self-Authority.

Variations. Lower gaze rather than cross eyes.

140. Upward to Space – Urdva Drishti

Chakras/Doshas/Vayus. Crown/All/Upward.

Cautions. Balance and neck conditions.

Benefits. Concentration, alignment, focus, and balance.

Cues. Gaze upwards without fixating on a point.

Sequence. Warrior I, Chair, Tall Mountain.

Variations. Lessen arch in neck, close eyes and internally gaze upward.

141. 3rd Eye – Brumadya Drishti

Chakras/Doshas/Vayus. 3rd Eye/All/Inward.

Cautions. Eye conditions, and can cause eye injury for anyone if straining

Benefits. Can elevate awareness, insight, and creativity. Activates pineal gland to improve melatonin and mood.

Cues. To learn, gaze inward at a pineconish light between eyebrows and behind forehead. Raise eyelids slightly and keep inward gaze (light may appear blue, violet, or white).

Sequence. Nadi Shodhana, Sat Kriya, Kirtan Kriya, default gaze in Kundalini.

Variations. Partially closed eyes.

142. Fingertip(s) – Hastagra Drishti

Chakras/Doshas/Vayus. Heart/All/Inward.

Cautions. None.

Benefits. Concentration, alignment, focus, and balance.

Cues. Gaze at hands or fingers in pose identified area of hand, such as thumb.

Sequence. Warrior II, Triangle, Extended Angle, Caliber of Life Meditation.

Variations. Keep eyes closed or open with internal gaze to 3rd Eye/brow point.

143. Right or Left Side – Parshva Drishti

Chakras/Doshas/Vayus. Not specific/All/Inward.

Cautions. Neck conditions.

Benefits. Concentration, alignment, focus, and balance.

Cues. Gaze follows movements to either side depending on pose.

Sequence. Revolved poses, Qigong movements, Washing Machine, Head Turns.

Variations. Lessen rotation of neck for more neutral gaze.

144. Navel – Nabi Drishti

Chakras/Doshas/Vayus. Solar/All/Inward.

Cautions. Eye and heart conditions.

Benefits. Concentration, alignment, focus, and balance.

Cues. Gaze at navel without straining.

Sequence. Downward Facing Dog, inversions, internal navel gaze in Sat Kriya.

Variations. Keep eyes closed with internal gaze to navel point.

145. Feet – Padagra Drishti

Chakras/Doshas/Vayus. Root/All/Downward.

Cautions. Pre-natal, osteoporosis and back conditions.

Benefits. Concentration, alignment, focus, and balance.

Cues. Gaze at feet or toes specific to pose cues.

Sequence. Forward Bends, Head to Knee, Stretch Pose.

Variations. Keep eyes closed with internal gaze to feet.

146. Top of the Head – Sahasara Drishti (also called 10th Gate)

Chakras/Doshas/Vayus. Crown/All/Inward, upward.

Cautions. Eye conditions.

Benefits. Elevated awareness, insight, and sense of universal connection. Can improve mood.

Cues. Close eyes, internally gaze at top of head as if there is a bright light at top of the head.

Sequence. Various meditations.

Variations. Begin with short periods of time and increase as comfortable.

147. Partially Closed Eyes Drishti (also called 1/10th)

Chakras/Doshas/Vayus. 3rd Eye/All/Inward.

Cautions. None.

Benefits. Promotes calmness, introspection, and focus.

Cues. Close eyes, then open them just enough to see light.

Sequence. Various meditations.

Variations. Combine this gaze with 3rd eye gaze.

148. Candle Gazing – Trataka Drishti

Chakras/Doshas/Vayus. Root/All/Inward.

Cautions. Eye conditions, epilepsy, or migraines.

Benefits. Promotes calmness and clarity, and can improve energy, health, memory, and sleep,

Cues. Darken practice area, light a candle approx. 2 ft away at eye level when seated.

Perform several rounds of segmented breath with 8 inhales to 4 exhales.

Open eyes to stare at tip of candle flame without blinking until impossible.

Finally, close eyes to bring image of flame behind eyelids until internal flame fades.

Sequence. This is one of Ayurveda's Shatkarmas or cleansing techniques.

Variations. Perform with eyes closed to focus on internal image of a flame or on an image of choice.

Bandhas (Locks)

"Mastering yourself is true power" — Lao Tzu.

Many yogic techniques reference bandhas, which are energy locks you can activate to temporarily build, halt and release energy flow. Applying bandhas can both increase physical stability and release emotional blockages by controlling energy within. For example, in the Ashtanga Primary Series during the transitioning from Downward Facing Dog to seated poses, there is a "hopping through" that is difficult and has potential for injury if bandhas are not engaged. And in many Kundalini kriyas, bandha control is key to the kriya's outcome. Additionally, bandhas provide a sense of internal control, regardless of what is occurring on the outside. Some important notes for Bandhas are:

- ✓ Some bandhas are not recommended for pregnancy, menstruation, abdominal and heart conditions..
- ✓ Cautions presented cannot cover all variables and are not a substitute for medical advice.

149. Hasta (Hands) Bandha

Chakras/Doshas/Vayus. Root/All/Inward.

Cautions. None.

Benefits. Can strengthen hands and wrists and reduce wrist and shoulder injuries.

Can increase circulation and inward focus.

Cues. Fingers spread wide, middle fingers points forward.

Press thumbs and knuckles/bases of fingers downward to create lift inside palm.

Sequence. Downward Facing Dog, Balancing Table, Plank.

Variations. Apply similar principles to available fingers or upper extremities.

150. Pada (Feet) Bandha

Chakras/Doshas/Vayus. Root/All/Inward.

Cautions. None.

Benefits. Can strengthen feet and ankles and reduce ankle and knee injuries.

Stabilizes body weight and promotes circulation and inward focus.

Cues. Spread toes, press corners of feet down (pads at big and pinky toes, and sides of heel).

Energetically lift foot arches upward to activate muscles in legs.

Sequence. Standing and balancing poses.

Variations. Apply similar principles to available toes or lower extremities.

151. Mula (Root) Bandha

Chakras/Doshas/Vayus. Root/All/Downward.

Cautions. Pre-natal and heavy menstruation.

Benefits. Can support stabilization of pelvic floor and lower core muscles.

Can promote digestion and increased energy.

Cues. Female bodies contract muscles at bottom of pelvic floor behind cervical area.

Male bodies contract area between anus and testes.

Engage inner muscles around contracted area upward to seal energy at lowest point.

Sequence. Transitions such as Chaturangas, and in many Kundalini kriyas and meditations.

Variations. Perform Kegel exercises.

152. Uddiyana (Fly) Bandha

Chakras/Doshas/Vayus. Solar/All/Balancing.

Cautions. Pre-natal, abdominal and heart conditions.

Benefits. Can strengthen abdominal muscles and core stability.

Offers uplifted ease in transitions.

Basics. Practice in Halfway Lift, draw navel inward towards spine and up towards ribs.

From any position, suspend breath out on exhale, draw navel inward and up toward ribs.

Sequence. In Ashtanga Seated Series, some inversions, and many Kundalini kriyas.

Variations. Perform gentle version by engaging inward and upward with assistance of an inhale.

153. Jalandhara (Throat Net) Bandha

Chakras/Doshas/Vayus. Throat/All/Elevating.

Cautions.   Heart, neck, and balance conditions.

Benefits.   Promotes concentration, stimulates thyroid, and spinal cord fluid.
Seals off energy in the torso from leaving through mouth, eyes, and ears.

Cues.   Easy Pose, hands on thighs, straight elbows, inhale through nose.
Tilt chin down, lift chest, engage top of throat muscles, curl tongue to roof of mouth.

Sequence.   Various meditations and Kundalini kriyas.

Variations.   Perform with little or no tilt in chin by engaging muscles at top of throat.

154. Maha (All Together) Bandha

Chakras/Doshas/Vayus. All/All/ Downward, balancing, elevating.

Cautions.   Pre-natal, heavy menstruation, heart, abdominal, balance and neck conditions.

Benefits.   Focuses internal energy, stimulates circulation, digestion, and respiratory processes.

Cues.   Easy Pose, inhale, and exhale fully through nose, then engage Mula Bandh.
Add Uddiyana Bandh, inhale again to lift chest, engaging Jalandhara Bandh.
To release, lift head, inhale fully, and release all bandhs.

Sequence.   Advanced meditation.

Variations.   Try doing the variations of all Mula, Uddiyana and Jalandhara.

Mudras (Gestures)

"Grace has been defined as the outward expression of the inward harmony of the soul"
- William Hazlitt.

Mudras, outward gestures of inward intention, are yet another yogic technique that can consciously impact energy. Mudras subtly impact the brain's autonomic nerve reflexes through energy circuits of the fingers, each of which represents an element that corresponds to a kosha and one or more vayus. Each finger may also represent a meridian. Kundalini kriyas often use mudras, further linking them to planetary connections.

Mudras are often added to poses, breathing techniques, and meditations to focus prana by subtly impacting energy circuits. For example, each of the five fingers represents one of the five elements that correspond to one of the koshas and one or more vayus, and depending on the tradition, each finger also represents a meridian and/or planetary influence. Some primary mudras are included here, but there are also many more to explore if you are interested. If you cannot utilize mudras for any reason, brainstorm other ways you might create similar energy circuits to influence the same vayu direction.

155. Prayer – Anjali Mudra (Anj = celebrate; ali = joining of palms)

Chakras/Doshas/Vayus. Heart/All/Inward, upward.

Cautions.   None.

Benefits.   Promotes left and right brain balance, centering, and focus.

Cues.   Left palm against right palm, all fingers touch to activate all 5 elements

Sequence.   Mountain, Tree, and various meditations.

Variations. Hands on heart.

156. Peace Fingers – Chin or Gyan Mudra (Chin = Consciousness; Gyan = Knowledge)

Chakras/Doshas/Vayus. 3rd Eye, Crown/All/Inward, upward.

Cautions.   Finger conditions.

Benefits.   Promotes concentration, memory, creativity.

Cues.   Index finger to thumb, other fingers are straight or slightly curved.

Sequence.   Mountain, Tree, and various meditations.

Variations. Palm up (Gyan) for openness and palm down (Chin) for grounding.

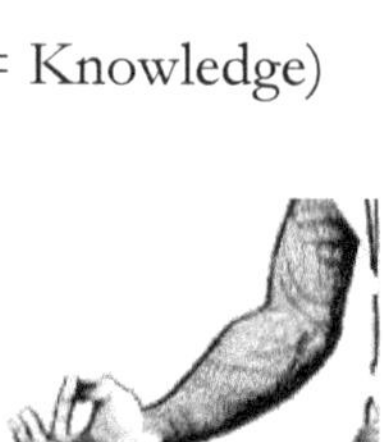

157. Akash - Shuni Mudra (Shuni = Patience; also called Akash = Space)

Chakras/Doshas/Vayus. Solar Plexus, Throat, 3rd Eye/All except excess Vata/Inward.

Cautions.   Finger conditions.

Benefits.   Promotes intuition, positivity, discipline, patience; migraine relief.

Cues.   Tip of thumb to tip of middle finger (enough pressure to feel connection).

Sequence.   Meditation, Pittra Kriya, can be added to poses such as Crescent Lunge.

Variations. Flick fingers to intensify effects.

158. Meditation Gesture - Dhyana Mudra (Dyana = Meditation)

Chakras/Doshas/Vayus. 3rd Eye, Crown/All/Inward, balancing.

Cautions.   None.

Benefits.   Promotes left and right brain balance, centering, and focus.

Cues.   Place left hand (illusion) on center of lap, palm up.

Place right hand (enlightenment) on top of the left hand.

Thumbs join softly, all fingers touch to activate all 5 elements

Sequence.   Meditation and pranayama practices.

Variations. Combine Gyan mudra with Dhyana, right long fingers aligning with left long fingers.

159. Hakini Mudra (Hakini = Power)

Chakras/Doshas/Vayus. Solar, Throat, 3rd Eye/All/Inward, downward, balancing.

Cautions.   Finger conditions.

Benefits.   Promotes brain balance, confidence, memory, expression.

Cues.   Palms of hands face, touch fingertips of hands.

All fingers touch to activate all 5 elements

Sequence.   Tattva Balance Meditation, prior to speaking.

Variations. Do an alternative mudra, such as Shuni or Prayer.

160. **Lotus - Padma Mudra** (Padma = Lotus)

Chakras/Doshas/Vayus. All/All/Inward, upward.

Cautions.   Finger conditions.
Benefits.   Promotes brain balance, compassion, and optimism.
Cues.   From Prayer, thumbs/pinky fingers together, open other fingers.
Sequence.   Meditation can be added to many poses and Qigong movements.
Variations.   Inhale Lotus overhead, exhale as palms flip, backs of wrist lower and repeat.

161. **Sun - Surya Mudra** (Surya = Sun; also known as Agni = Fire Mudra)

Chakras/Doshas/Vayus. Solar/All except excess Pitta/ Inward, downward, expanding.

Cautions.   Finger conditions and high temperatures.
Benefits.   Promotes focus, clarity, energy, heat; stimulates digestion and metabolism.
Cues.   Thumb tips to 2nd joint of ring fingers (enough pressure to feel connection).
                   If thumb cannot reach joint without bending fingers, adjust pressure point.
Sequence.   To generate heat.
Variations.   Other mudras that generate heat such as Shiva Mudra.

162. **Buddhi Mudra** (Buddhi = intellect)

Chakras/Doshas/Vayus. Solar, 3rd Eye /All/ Inward, downward.

Cautions.   None.
Benefits.   Promotes vision, focus and clarity; stimulates digestion and elimination.
Cues.   Press tips of pinkies to tips of thumbs, other fingers remain straight.
Sequence.   Meditation, or added to poses such as Crescent Lunge.
Variations.   Thumb on nail of pinky finger and other fingers slightly curved.

Mantra (Chants)

As I walked through the corridors of the infinite and nameless,
the candle in my heart whispered, "welcome home."

All yogic practices can act as a compass to inner alignment. But the human brain loves to return to its pre-programmed place when not actively engaged in those practices. Using mantra is a tool for your brain when it is making a beeline for places it likes to go that aren't serving you. Mantra can be a new map for thoughts to explore, a place existing beyond time and space. Mantra repetition brings the present moment into focus with the resonation of sound, while promoting a sense of deep connection even when alone.

Known origins of each mantra included in this section can help you navigate what you may or may not be comfortable with to begin. Some mantras included here come from Sikh tradition - which believes in one creator, unity, equality of all, selfless service, social justice, and honest conduct and active livelihood based upon truthfulness, creativity, self-control, and purity. There is no dogma that says people who are not Sikhs cannot practice their mantras or that if they do, they are somehow transformed into a devotee.

Other mantras include chanting names that may be recognized as Hindu deities in some religions. Most mantras here originated prior to organized religion and are presented thus so. This book's companion, *The Guru is You: Yoga for Self-Discovery and Purposeful Living*, offers storytelling interlaced with mantras.

Continued mantra practice can yield significant benefits that perpetuate over time. All mantras in this book are meant to be tried as repetitions of the same words for at least three minutes. Phonetic spelling of these mantras is not provided here as applying phonetic exercises is not usually preferable to learning mantra by repetition from a teacher. You can search the mantras on a music streaming service to hear the pronunciation in a way that most resonates with you. Pronunciation may feel awkward, but continued practice with intention can yield great benefit. The Kundalini yoga lineage offers guidelines for the length of time to recite mantra or practice kriyas (see Kundalini under Other Poses and Practices).

163. Ashtanga Opening

Meaning. I bow at the lotus feet of the guru who teaches knowledge of self-awakening.

Like a jungle doctor going in to remove poison of the ignorance of conditioned existence.

The upper body holds a conch, discus and sword, has a thousand heads of white light.

I bow to Patanjali. I seal my offering with the sound of infinite wisdom and connection.

Benefits. Denotes an embarking on a journey, where your practice is an opportunity for self-awakening, removal of toxins, gratitude for the sages and freedom.

Origin. This mantra is from *The Yogatārāvalī*, written around 1400 CE on Hatha and Raja Yoga and cited in the *Hatha Yoga Pradipika.*

Mantra. Om, Vande Gurunam Charanaravinde

Sandarshita Svatma Sukava Bodhe

Nih Sreyase Jangalikayamane

Samsara Halahala Mohashantyai

Abahu purusakaram

Shankachakrasi dharinam

Sahasra sirasam svetam

Pranamami Patanjalim, Om

Sequence. First verse of the opening chant of the Ashtanga sequence. Typically, the entire mantra (not included here) begins class as a call and response between teacher and students.

Or begin practice with other words that remind you to infuse practice with intention, resolve, gratitude, and awareness.

164. Ashtanga Closing

Meaning. May rulers keep to the path of virtue and protect the welfare of all generations.

May all peoples be forever blessed; may all beings everywhere be happy and free.

In infinite wisdom and connection, peace, peace, perfect peace.

Benefit. Promotes a sense of universal connection and peace.

Origin. From *The Yogatārāvalī*, written around 1400 CE on Hatha and Raja Yoga.

Mantra. Om, Svasthi Praja Bhyaha Pari Pala Yantam

Nya Yena Margena Mahim Mahishaha

Go Brahmanebhyaha Shubamastu Nityam

Lokah Samastah Sukhino Bhavantu

Om, Shanti Shanti Shantihi

Sequence. The last verse of closing chant of the Ashtanga sequence, performed as call and response. You can also seal your practice in another wish for happiness, freedom, and peace.

165. Adi Mantra

Meaning. I bow to the divine teacher within.

Guru – One who brings light to darkness. Ong Namo - Oh creative total self.

Benefits. Acknowledges the great teachers in your life, living and past.

Origin. Taught by Guru Ram Das, who lived in the 1500s, and was the first successor to Guru Nanak, the founder of the Sikh tradition.

Mantra. Ong Namo Guru Dev Namo

Sequence. Kundalini yoga classes often open by chanting this mantra 3 times.

Or use other words that honors your presence and gives gratitude to your lessons, your tradition, and your inner teacher.

166. Mangala Charn

Meaning. I bow to primal wisdom through the ages, to true wisdom, to the great, unseen wisdom. The wisdom within is beyond imagination.

Benefits. Can increase mindfulness during practice.

Origin. Mangalacharn is used in Vedic texts as an introduction to a teaching.

It originated with Guru Arjun Dev Ji, the 5th Sikh guru,

who composed 2,000+ hymns in the late 1500s.

Mantra. Aad Guray Nameh, Jugaad Guray Nameh, Sat Guray Nameh, Siri Guru Dayvay Nameh

Sequence. Typically, the 2nd chant in Kundalini practice after Adi Mantra, and it is chanted either once or 3 times, and sometimes in all 4 directions.

Or say another set of words that represents placing an imaginary necklace of protection over you before you begin any endeavor.

167. Long Time Sun

Meaning. A wish or prayer of blessings for others.

Benefits. Promotes sense of goodwill and community.

Origin. Written by Mike Heron, recorded by the Incredible String Band, and sung by Paul Joseph from Australia in the 1960s during a meeting for the Kundalini Aquarius Festival.

Mantra. May the long time sun shine upon you, all love surround you, and the pure light within you, guide your way on.

Sequence. Typically used as a Kundalini practice closing mantra.

Or use another set of words, such as Metta meditation, to offer good wishes for others.

168. Sat Nam

Meaning. Truth is my identity/name.

Benefits. Affirms the qualities of strength, goodness, and ability to prosper within ourselves.

Origin. Though both Sat and Nam appear in the same contexts used in this mantra in ancient Vedic texts, the mantra's use in this way likely originated with Guru Nanak in 1469.

Mantra. Sat Nam

Sequence. Typically, the final chant after Kundalini practice, and also used as an acknowledgement affirming truth in others. Or use other words that honor the essence in all sentient beings.

169. Ang Sung Wahe Guru

Meaning. Ang = cell; Sang = every part; Wahe = ecstasy (or wow!); Guru = inner teacher (or God)

Benefits. Can shift negativity and feelings of separateness to joy of connection with all that is.

Origin. Uncertainty exists as to the source, though it is derived from the Sikh tradition.

Mantra. Ang Sang Wahe Guru

Sequence. To experience inner warmth, positivity and to initiate creative projects.

Or use another set of words to remind you that beyond your ego, ecstasy exists in your cells and that joy is waiting to shine.

170. Ganesha

Meaning. Salutations to Ganesha.

Benefits. Affirms the qualities of strength, goodness, and ability to prosper within ourselves.

Origin. Ganesha, also called Ganapati, has origins in the Rig Veda where Ganesha becomes known for attributes of speech, writing, math, scientific knowledge, love, kindness, security, and stability.

Mantra. Om Gam Ganapataye Namaha

Sequence. To remove negativity before beginning something important.

Or use other words that remind you that even smarts and muscles can't beat negativity, which can be the greatest obstacle.

171. Green Tara

Meaning. Enlightenment and liberation from eight spiritual fears, let this mantra embed in me.

Benefits. Can promote a sense of resilience and trust that the universe has "got your back."

Origin. Green Tara is found in Tibetan Buddhism and Tantra around 600 CE as the mother of liberation who offers protection to sentient beings facing difficulty.

Mantra. Om Tara Tuttare Ture Svaha

Sequence. To remind yourself of inner resources that you possess of intellect, humility, equanimity, tranquility, altruism, action, contentment, and trust that always offer protection.

Or use other words that remind you that the universe is conspiring for you.

172. Saraswati

Meaning. Salutations to Saraswati.

Benefits. Can promote learning and creativity.

Origin. In the Mahabharata, Saraswati is the mother of the Vedas who composes a symphony, and in the Rig Veda, she is an avatar endowed with the power of abundant water who symbolizes our innate capacities to learn, create and express our inner truths.

Mantra. Om Aing Saraswati Namah

Sequence. To remind you of your qualities of truth, creation, memory, power, and concentration.

Or use other words to tune into your capacity to learn, create, and express yourself.

173. Sita Ram

Meaning. Victory to Sita and Ram!

Benefits. Affirms the qualities of courage, devotion, integrity, and peace within you.

Origin. In the Ramayana, the avatar Rama is the main character hero in the face of adversity. Sita is Rama's beloved, whose courage and devotion keep her safe even though she walks through fire.

Mantra. Sita Ram, Sita Ram, Sita Ram, Jaya Sita Ram

Sequence. To remember that trials may come, but courage and internal peace will see you through. Or use other words to affirm integrity and internal peace regardless of circumstances

174. Maha Mantra

Meaning. Calling on the source of wisdom to remove illusion.

Benefits. Promotes a sense of inner and radiant bliss by affirming the qualities of devoted compassion, love, and tenderness within ourselves that are the source of expanded consciousness.

Origin. Found in the Kali-Santarana Upanishad, written around 500 CE. It includes 8 syllables that are said to vibrate and resonate in such a way that higher levels of consciousness and divine realization can be experienced. The avatar Krishna is most known for his role in the Bhagavad Gita, where he takes on the incarnation of Brahman to represent the presence of transcendent wisdom in all situations.

Mantra. Hare Rama Hare Rama
Rama Rama Hare Hare
Hare Krishna Hare Krishna
Krishna Krishna Hare Hare

Sequence. To remind yourself that compassion to yourself and others expands wisdom and joy. Or choose another set of words that promotes expanding love and consciousness. Followers of the International Society for Krishna Consciousness repeat this mantra silently in Japa and out loud in Kirtan.

175. Om Shree Sache

Meaning. May truth beyond all boundaries be victorious. May there be peace, peace, peace.

Benefits. Promotes feelings of love, connection, and goodwill.

Origin. Uncertainty exists as to the source of this mantra, though it is derived from Sikh tradition.

Mantra. Om shree saché maha prabhu ki jai.
Paramatma ki jai.
Om shanti shanti shantihi om.

Sequence. Whenever you want to promote experience the expansiveness of the heart. Or use another set of words that affirm the boundless nature of love and peace.

176. Antar Naad (Antar = inner; Naad = sound that transcends languages; also Kabadshe Meditation)

> **Meaning.** Sa – Infinite; Re (connecting note)
>
> Har – Creativity (power of manifestation)
>
> Rung – Complete totality
>
> Infinity is everywhere. Creativity is everywhere.
>
> **Benefits.** Affirms present awareness, calms mind and body, stimulates the spine and Sushumna channel and prepares the chakra centers for further practice.
>
> **Origin.** Uncertainty exists as to the source, though Antar Naad is basic to the Sikh tradition.
>
> **Mantra.** Sa Re Sa Sa, Sa Re Sa Sa, Sa Re Sa Sa, Sa Rung
>
> Har Re Har Har, Har Re Har Har, Har Re Har Har, Har Rung
>
> **Sequence.** Use to affirm infinite wisdom with and around you. To add mudra, begin with hands in prayer mudra in front of the lower abdomen. As you chant the first half of the mantra, raise your hands and open the fingers to lotus mudra at heart level and continue raising your lotus upward to the 3rd eye. At the end of the first verse and at the top of your mudra, flip your hands so wrists touch and move hands down for 2nd verse back to prayer mudra at abdomen.

177. Sa Ta Na Ma

> **Meaning.** Sa–infinity; Ta-life, existence; Na-death, totality, transition;
>
> Ma-rebirth, resurrection, re-creation
>
> **Benefits.** Provides a reminder that every moment is temporary and connected and we are only and always experiencing one form of the cycle of the truth of life.
>
> **Origin.** Though both Sat and Nam appear in ancient Vedic texts, the mantra's use in this way likely originated with Guru Nanak, founder of the Sikh tradition in 1469.
>
> **Mantra.** Sa Ta Na Ma Ra Ma Da Sa Sa Se So Hung
>
> **Sequence.** As a reminder that life is a cycle and our natural state is change.
>
> Or choose other words to affirm this circle of life.

178. Ra Ma Da Sa – Siri Gatri

> **Meaning.** Ra - sun and connecting/energy
>
> Ma - moon/receptivity
>
> Da – Earth/grounding
>
> Sa - Infinity/Universe
>
> Say - All-encompassing Thou
>
> So Hung - Merging essence of creation / I am thou
>
> **Benefits.** Stimulates the spine, the sushumna energy channel and opens chakra centers.
>
> **Origin.** Includes consonants of Sanskrit alphabet, though uncertainty exists as to source.
>
> **Mantra.** Ra Ma Da Sa, Sa Say So Hung
>
> **Sequence.** As a reminder that human life is also part of nature and merged with something greater.
>
> Or chant this while you mentally visualize an issue or someone you wish to send prayers or good intentions to, then visualize a white light around the issue or person.

179. Ong So Hung

Meaning. I am one with universal consciousness.

Benefits. Promotes compassion, inner guidance, and a sense of elevated awareness.

Origin. Found in the Upanishads in reference to humans needing not only a material life, but also a spiritual one.

Mantra. Ong So Hung

Sequence. Chant this mantra to remind yourself that you are not alone or separate and wish to inspire a sense of being part of something larger than yourself.

Or chant a shorter mantra with similar meaning, "So Hum."

180. Gayatri (is often referred to as the mother of all mantras)

Meaning. Om – Infinite; Bhur – Existence; Bhuvah – Consciousness; Suvah – Bliss

Tat – that; Savitur – Creator; Varenyam – Adore

Bhargo – Divine Light; Devasya – Supreme; Dhimahi - Meditate

Dhiyo – Buddhi; Yo – May this Light; Na – Our; Prachodayat - Illume

Benefits. Can lower cortisol levels and neutralize stress.

Origin. First shows up as a song with 24 meters in the Rig Veda, later in the Chandogya Upanishad and Mahabharata, and even later in Puranas.

Gayatri also denotes the meter of recitation.

Mantra. Om

Bhur Bhuvah Suvah

Tat Savitur Varenyam

Bargo Devasya Dhimahi

Dhiyo Yo Nah Prachodayat

Sequence. Whenever there is doubt as to which mantra to use. Try imagining the sun's rays streaming into the world, into your heart, then streaming out from your center as blessings to the world. Or use other words that remind that your experience of existence can go beyond the body.

181. Om Mani Padme Hum

Meaning. Embodied practice can transform ordinary thought and actions into exalted ones like that of a buddha, or the "jewel is in the lotus."

Benefits. Can settle the mind and open the heart.

Origin. Originated in the early years of the current era as part of the Mahayana sutras which correlate to ancient Vedic texts and the rise of Buddhism.

Mantra. Om Mani Padme Hum

Sequence. Repeat this mantra whenever calming is needed to access wisdom. It can be especially powerful for Vatas. You can also combine this mantra with a Buddhist prayer wheel or use another set of words to remind you that beyond your thoughts, your inner being is an untarnishable jewel of love and compassion.

182. Har Mokunday – Magnificent Mantra

Meaning. Gobinday – Sustainer; Mokunday – Liberator; Udaaray – Enlightener; Apaaray – Infinite; Hariang – Destroyer; Kariang – Creator; Nirnaamay – Nameless; Akaamay – Desireless; Har – Infinite or God

Benefits. Can heighten inner guidance (chant the "r" in Har with tongue to the palette to stimulate the pituitary gland) and courage to do the work needed to prosper.

Origin. Uncertainty exists as to the source, though it is derived from the Sikh tradition.

Mantra. Har Har Har Har Gobinday

Har Har Har Har Mokunday

Har Har Har Har Udaaray

Har Har Har Har Apaaray

Har Har Har Har Hariang

Har Har Har Har Kariang

Har Har Har Har Nir-naamay

Har Har Har Har Akaamay

Sequence. Chant this mantra whenever you want to get out of the way of prosperity coming your way. Or use other words that promotes a sense of inner radiance and inner alignment.

183. Ho'opononopo (Ho'opononopo = to correct/cleanse)

Meaning. Forgiveness prayer.

Benefits. Can support release of internal hurts to heighten self-love and compassion for others.

Origin. From a Polynesian belief that illness and anger cause sickness, so these words act as a Hawaiian reconciliation practice for wellness.

Mantra. I'm sorry. Please forgive me. Thank you. I love you.

Sequence. Part of a daily meditation to allow internal hurt that resides within you to experience its source (often it is self-blame that is the deepest). You can also follow the entire process used in families or communities for reconciliation by stating the problem, discussing the transgression without assigning blame, allowing silence and reflection, acknowledging feelings of those involved, and releasing feelings of anger or hurt.

184. Bliss – Ananda Hum (Ananda = Bliss; Hum = I am)

Meaning. I am bliss.

Benefits. Promotes awareness of spiritual self and connection to other's essences, which are also bliss.

Origin. Uncertainty exists as to the source, though it is derived from the Sikh tradition.

Mantra. I am the light of my soul,

I am beautiful, I am bountiful, I am bliss.

I am. I am.

Sequence. Anytime you wish to glow from the inside out. This is also a great mantra to use in a large group practice of people from all backgrounds as a celebration of spirit.

185. Seed Sounds – Bija Mantras (Bija = Seed)

Meaning. Each syllable resonates with specific internal energy and a body part or region.

Benefits. Improve focus, relaxation, and support internal alignment.

Origin. Found in the Rig and Sama Vedas. Later Tantric texts associate the syllables to chakras.

Mantra. Lam - Root

Vam - Sacral

Ram – Solar Plexus

Yam - Heart

Ham - Throat

Om – 3rd Eye

Aum - Crown

Sequence. You can focus on one Bija, repeating it over and over; or you can chant them all in order – letting each sound reverberate in your body and noticing where you most feel that sound. Or say the rights of each chakra center, though sounds will not vibrate on the physical level.

186. OM / AUM

Meaning. OM is the primal sound of the universe.

Benefits. Can increase present moment awareness and calm mind and body.

Origin. Found in ancient texts of the Rig and Sama Vedas, the later texts of the Vedantas, in the Epics and in *The Yoga Sutras*, and in virtually every text on the philosophy and science of yoga since.

Mantra. OM (or AUM)

Sequence. Many yoga classes begin and/or end with chanting of OM.

You can also hum or use another word for self-alignment and infinite connection.

Guided Meditations

Enjoy the play in Prakriti (human playground) but know you are not that.

In yoga, you have achieved meditation (the limb of Dhyana) when you go beyond any concepts of time or space or body. Practicing the other limbs of yoga helps to understand the value of meditation and be ready for it, but in my experience the only thing that makes meditation easier is meditation.

There are various ways to prepare for it, such as walking meditation and guided meditation, but nothing substitutes sitting still with yourself and connecting to your breath long enough to attain that which is otherwise unattainable. How long is long enough depends on how many times you practice sitting with yourself in silence. The more it becomes a habit, the easier and quicker it becomes to experience this gift each time you begin.

Patanjali's yoga sutra 1.02. states that yoga is the cessation of the fluctuations of the mind (any thought not of your true essential nature). Sitting with yourself in silence – mind, body, and spirit – as one, is the goal of yoga. While other wisdom traditions discuss optional ways of meditating, yoga specifies it as a state of nothingness to oneness. Meditation, the state of doing nothing, is perhaps the hardest thing to do.

Try practicing meditation by setting a timer for 1 minute for a few days, then 3 minutes for a few days, then 5 minutes and so on. The more silent and still meditation becomes a habit, the easier and quicker it becomes to experience instant benefits each time you begin. Seated meditation is recommended, if possible, as sitting with a straight spine allows a natural and focused energy flow. However, you can perform meditation in any position of stillness. If silence feels intolerable, listening to binaural beats while meditating can be beneficial.

Meditation is tri-doshic and there is no risk of injury. And as far as chakras, though meditation is typically seated and so is a root chakra posture with downward energy, meditation most impacts chakra balance in heart, throat, 3rd Eye and crown chakras that results in inward and upward energy.

The benefits of meditation are widely acclaimed and include improved cognitive function, sense of inner alignment and resilience, sleep, stress reduction, and pain control. And adding meditation to any asana practice provides an element of ritual, relaxation, and observation. Meditation can be even more potent at the start and finish of each day. Once meditation practice has been established, it can be employed anywhere at any time as a superpower of sorts to live your most meaningful life.

In yoga, you have achieved meditation when you go beyond any concepts of time or space or body. Guided meditation can help prepare one for actual meditation, so several guided options are included here.

187. Breath Awareness

Cues. Lengthen spine, rest hands, or choose mudra, close eyes or choose drishti.

With no attempt to regulate breath, notice sensations in torso during natural breathing.

Mind follows the breath in and out, noticing sensations of breath.

When mind becomes distracted, focus it again on inhales and exhales.

188. Gratitude Meditation

Cues. Place left hand on heart, bend right elbow at right side so palm is up in front of body.

Lengthen spine, close eyes, or gaze at tip of nose.

Inhale slowly through nose, exhale softly through open mouth "O" toward your palm.

To finish, bring hands in front of heart, palms cupped/stacked as if to receive a gift.

Imagine the universe pouring gifts into your hands, then open your eyes and witness the gifts around you.

189. Chakra Meditation

Cues. Inhale Red Light and the security of Earth, into the tailbone, the Root Chakra.

Exhale Red Light from the tailbone. I AM SAFE. I have a right to be here.

Inhale Orange Light and the creativity of Water into the pelvis, the Sacral Chakra.

Exhale Orange Light from the pelvis. I AM AUTHENTIC. I have a right to feel.

Inhale Yellow Light and the strength of fire into the navel area, the Solar Plexus Chakra.

Exhale Yellow Light from the navel area. I AM CONFIDENT. I have a right to act.

Inhale Green Light and the softness of AIR, into the chest, the Heart Chakra.

Exhale Green Light from the chest. I AM LOVE. I have a right to unconditional love.

Inhale Blue Light and the clarity of space, into the throat, the Throat Chakra.

Exhale Blue Light from the throat. I AM TRUTH. I have a right to speak and be heard.

Inhale Indigo Light and the vision of night sky in between eyebrows, 3rd Eye Chakra.

Exhale Indigo Light from between the eyebrows. I AM TRUST. I have a right to know.

Inhale Violet Light and universal consciousness to the top of head, the Crown Chakra.

Exhale Violet Light from the top of head. I AM CONNECTED. I have a right to unity.

190. Metta Meditation

Cues. Breathe naturally and repeat the words out loud or internally.

Think of yourself and your well-being. *(Repeat the following 3x)*.

May I be happy. May I feel healthy. May I experience peace. May I know freedom.

Now consider someone that you know and love. *(Repeat the following 3x)*.

May you be happy. May you feel healthy. May you experience peace. May you know freedom.

Now consider someone whom you cannot understand. *(Repeat the following 3x)*.

May you be happy. May you feel healthy. May you experience peace. May you know freedom.

Now consider all beings. *(Repeat the following 3x)*.

May all beings be happy. May all beings feel healthy. May all beings experience peace.

May all beings know freedom. May this practice benefit the goodness of all humanity.

191. Inner Smile

Cues.   Clasp hands lightly, touch the tongue to roof of the mouth.

Relax forehead and eyes and imagine a smile or a sight that helps you smile.

Allow feelings of happiness and beauty in your forehead to expand in a pleasurable glow.

Breathe that smile energy into your forehead, eyebrows, nose, and cheeks to relax your skin and to penetrate the facial muscles as it warms the whole face like sunshine.

Float that smiling energy to your jaw, releasing tension.

Continue smiling energy to your neck and throat, filling it with soft Golden Light.

Every inhale invites more light and golden smile energy inside.

The golden smile energy is flowing from your throat into your thyroid, thymus, heart, lungs, liver, kidneys, pancreas, spleen, and reproductive organs.

The golden smile flows generously through the esophagus, small intestine, and colon.

Return to follow golden smile energy upward to the 3rd Eye, pituitary gland, thalamus, pineal gland, and into the whole brain.

Golden energy spills down your back, stopping at each vertebra with a warm smile.

Every cell in the body is a joyful waterfall of smiles.

Your whole body is loved and appreciated.

Imagine collecting all the golden smile energy into a pot of gold near your navel.

Place your hands over your lower abdomen to feel the warm, happy glow.

192. Prayer for Peace Meditation

Cues.   Breathe naturally and repeat the following out loud or internally.

Light before me, light behind me.

Light at my left, light at my right.

Light below me, light above me.

Light within me, light unto me.

Light through me, light use me.

Light to all, I am light.

Peace before me, peace behind me.

Peace at my left, peace at my right.

Peace below me, peace above me.

Peace within me, peace unto me.

Peace through me, peace use me.

Peace to all, I am peace.

Love before me, love behind me.

Love at my left, love at my right.

Love below me, love above me.

Love within me, love unto me.

Love through me, love use me.

Love to all, I am love.

To finish, inhale and suspend breath to bring awareness to light, peace, and love within and around you. Exhale completely. Return to natural breath.

193. Kirtan Kriya (Kirtan = narrating or reciting)

Cues.   Chant Sa Ta Na Ma (a's are soft/long) in time with moving hand mudra for 12 minutes.
(0-2 min loudly, 2-4 min softly, 4-8 min silently, 8-10 min softly, 10-12 min loudly).
Gaze at an imaginary "L" beginning at the top of head and ending at 3rd Eye.
On Sa, thumb touches index finger (Gyan mudra).
On Ta, thumb touches middle finger (Shuni mudra).
On Na, thumb touches ring finger (Surya mudra).
On Ma, thumb touches pinky finger (Buddhi mudra).

194. Shabad Kriya for Sleep (Shabad = word or sound or spiritual poem)

Cues.   Hands in lap, palms up, right palm over left, thumbs touch and point away from body.
Gaze at tip of nose.
Inhale 4 segments of breath while mentally repeating Kirtan Kriya – Sa Ta Na Ma.
Suspend breath in and mentally repeat the mantra 4 times – Sa Ta Na Ma.
Exhale 2 segments of breath while mentally repeating Wahe Guru.
Repeat for 7 minutes or longer.

*C*hapter *5*

Fusion Class

My head, heart, and body take the first conscious breath.

And I meet myself there in that knowing,

That what I long for exists within me.

The Fusion Method as a simplified and reliable way to sequence mental, physical, and energetic wellness into yogic practices. This method involves 5 parts:

1. Identify an authentic focus area (what needs attention).
2. Create substance using the Koshas (layers of support).
3. Add musculoskeletal basics (physical functionality).
4. Categorize your substance (organize choices).
5. Sequence #4 into a Fusion Framework (sequence and test).

#2 above refers to Ayurveda's Koshic model (physical, energetic, mental, wisdom and bliss layers of being). This book's companion, *The Guru is You: Yoga for Self-Discovery and Purposeful Living,* offers deep exploration into koshic wisdom, as well as helpful information on the other steps in this method.

The basic class format on the following pages is offered to support your creation of a well-rounded one-hour yoga class or personal practice. Adjust sections lengths for the time of class or practice you desire.
If you add music to group classes, please research music copyright information.

Fusion Method Framework

Tuning In *(1-3 minutes)*

Tune in to acknowledge a transition from external focus to self-care.

Music/Sound: Om, another mantra, or no sound and inward intention.

Presence *(3-5 minutes)*

Establish presence with a breathing technique and simple movements to prepare joints and energy to expand upon.

Music/Sound: Simple rhythms that complement breath are ideal. Music here can introduce the overall class theme but should not detract from present moment awareness.

Engagement *(5-10 minutes)*

Engage mind and body towards your focus in functional and somatic ways (try pose variations as building blocks).

Music/Sound: Reinforce mental focus with music expressing universal challenges (different than songs with lyrics that promote triggers or attachments).

Flow *(15-30 minutes)*

Flow refers to energy momentum and need not mean Vinyasa. For example, when sequencing for Yin, flow refers to linking poses together with the least amount of physical adjustment from one pose to the next.

If vinyasa is used for Flow, start with basic poses that link easily and are held for 5 full breaths each (both sides), providing time for concise cues and an experience of healthy alignment. In subsequent repetitions, 1-3 new poses can be added each time. All repeated poses are synced to breath, and all new poses are held for 5 inhales and exhales the first time through for cueing and body connection. Transitions between poses are fluid and synced to breath to maintain energy movement. A flow may be 2-5 progressive rounds with transitions that are fluid.

Music/Sound: Promote inner agency. If Vinyasa, rhythms are slower pace in longer held poses and faster as movements become linked by breath. If a kriya is used, music may be fast or slow depending on kriya movements.
If Qigong is used, music with nature sounds and without words is the most complementary.

Edge *(5-10 minutes)*

The edge, if desired, offers a challenge to move past perceived limitations, such as a peak pose, or a short kriya.

Music/Sound: Music uncommon for other parts of a yoga class fits well. Could also encourage playing of instruments or audible sounds.

Release *(5-7 minutes)*

Decompress physical tension built during practice and allow wisdom to rise to the surface.

Repeating basic elements (in presence or engage) and a meditation or mantra, in addition to targeted musculoskeletal soothing can round out class focus and allows a sense of full-circle.

Music/Sound: Slow and simple music or mantra can support decompression and space for inner wisdom.
Lyrics used should reinforce your theme in a positive, universal ways.

Savasana/Rest/Integrate *(5-10 minutes)*

Time for being rather than doing.

Preparations for comfort have occurred prior for seamless transition to promote the subtle experience of bliss.

Music/Sound: Slow and simple with minimal, if any, words.

Lyrics that bring up a problem and tense, fast or loud sounds can interfere with an otherwise good experience.

Closing *(1-3 minutes)*

Acknowledge being present for oneself. Certain schools of yoga offer closing mantras.

Other classes end with Om, or a moment of gratitude.

Music/Sound: Acknowledges completion of a practice, like a short mantra or a few hums of a singing bowl are great options.

Fusion Method Template

You will likely need additional space than what is provided in this template.

Tuning In
    Duration   ____________________________
    Intention or Mantra   ____________________________

Presence
    Duration   ____________________________
    Concise theme introduction   ____________________________
    Breath technique to prepare mind   ____________________________
    Simple pose(s) to connect mind-body   ____________________________

Engagement
    Duration   ____________________________
    Cues for concise theme expansion   ____________________________
    Breath/energetic aids to build energy   ____________________________
    Engage joints/muscles/alignment   ____________________________

Flow
    Duration   ____________________________
    Cues - concise theme reinforcement   ____________________________
    Breath/energetic aids for class focus   ____________________________
    Type (vinyasa, yin, chakra, dosha, etc.)   ____________________________
    Poses (with transitions to link poses)   ____________________________

Edge
    Duration   ____________________________
    Cue - concise theme reinforcement   ____________________________
    Breathing technique(s)/energetic aids   ____________________________
    Peak pose or kriya   ____________________________

Release
    Duration   ____________________________
    Cue - concise theme affirmation   ____________________________
    Breathing technique/energetic aids   ____________________________
    Poses to soothe tension   ____________________________
    Meditation or mantra   ____________________________

Savasana/Rest/Integrate)
    Duration   ____________________________
    Preparations for comfort   ____________________________

Closing
    Duration   ____________________________
    Closing method and/or mantra   ____________________________

Total duration = __________

Note: Determine if accessibility plans are necessary prior to offering the class you prepared to others.

Chapter 6

Chakras, Doshas, Vayus

Theory without practice doesn't work,
And neither does practice without awareness.

This book is streamlined for practical use; however, this book's companion, *The Guru is You: Yoga for Self-Discovery and Purposeful Living*, offers further depth and self-study into Ayurveda and the Chakra system if desired.

Meanwhile, these quizzes can heighten awareness of individual needs for more specificity in determining which yogic techniques to utilize in class or practice sequencing. It is recommended to take multiple quizzes (on-line free quizzes are also available) to compare results and to consult experts in these areas for further support and guidance. Quizzes in this chapter include:

Constitution *(Prakriti, referred to commonly as Dosha, elemental forces in mind-body nature from birth)*

Imbalance *(Vikruti, subtle energy blockages arising from disrupters to one's natural state)*

Chakra Map *(to locate where blockages to energy might be housed)*

The last pages of this chapter identify Hatha methods that can support balance in specific areas pertaining to subtle energy in your Constitution and Chakras. Also included is a list of primary Vayus (directions of energy flow) and how differing Vayus can be used to achieve greater harmony in yoga classes and practices.

Constitution / Prakriti Quiz

Check one block for each area that best describes you for most of your life. The only right answer is the one that best describes you in your natural state, and there is not a best type of Dosha, all are needed equally. Most areas will have only one clear answer that is most like you. Rarely there may be more than one with equal prevalence in your natural state.   Sum up your checkmarks at the bottom.

In checking the block for each area, try to answer based upon times when you were NOT:

☒ experiencing rapid growth (childhood)

☒ experiencing fluctuating hormones (menstrual cycle, pre/post-natal or other, menopause)

☒ experiencing a new condition which caused a marked change that was abnormal for you

☒ trying to fit into a group or sport or reach a fitness goal (altering bodies temporarily)

When you have totaled your checkmarks, the totals will likely point to a Dosha that you naturally have the most elemental likeness to. Using that Dosha, along with any Imbalance you uncover in the next quiz, use the Dosha Basics for yogic techniques toward increased vitality in your mind and body.

Area	Vata (Air & Ether)		Pitta (Fire & Water)		Kapha (Earth & Water)	
Body Structure	Tends toward leaner, longer		Tends toward moderate size		Tends toward larger size	
Joints	Flexible		Stable		Round, well-developed	
Muscles	Small except arms		Naturally muscular		Firm but not defined	
Skin	Thin		Soft		Glowing	
Hair	Dry and fine		Medium structure		Thick and wavy	
Teeth	Small jaw prone to tooth decay		Mostly good prone to yellowing		Strong and white	
Hunger	Variable		Dependable		Low and steady	
Sweat	Very slow to sweat		Excessive		Minimal	
Sleep	Wakes easily		Sleeps easily unless hot		Sleeps hard, difficult to wake	
Digestion	Often constipated		Often regular		Often slow	
Activity	Quick to act		Likes competition		Slow but enduring	
Expression	Creative, playful, innovative		Strategic, productive,		Easy-going, forgiving, reliable	
In Stress	Overwhelm		Critical		Feeling hurt	
Memory	Good short-term		Sharp		Slow, but dependable	
Interests	Talking, moving		Debate, sports		Collecting, family gatherings	
Weather	Dislikes cold and wind		Aggravated in high heat		Sluggish in very cold and wet	
Action Starts With	Thinking		Doing		Feeling	
Totals	**Vata**		**Pitta**		**Kapha**	

Current Imbalance / Vikruti Quiz

Check one or more blocks for each area that best describes what is showing up consistently in the last 1-12 months in your mind and body. These are issues that you are dealing with that seem to decrease your vitality. You may somehow feel you deserve these issues because of lifestyle choices, but many people have a high level of imbalance for much longer than 1-12 months because of simply trying to do life with the information available. Include checking blocks for areas where you are currently under doctor's care for, even if it is managed by street or over-the-counter drugs, medical equipment, mental health therapy, surgery, or medication. Total your numbers at the bottom.

When you have totaled your checkmarks, the totals will likely point to an Imbalance reflecting elemental properties in your mind and body that may be disrupting your energy. Using that Imbalance, along with your Dosha from the previous quiz, you can use the Dosha Basics for yogic techniques toward increased vitality in your mind and body.

Area	Vata (Air & Ether)		Pitta (Fire & Water)		Kapha (Earth & Water)	
Joints/Muscles	Less strength and structure		Increased tension		Feeling increasingly heavy	
Skin	Dry		Early balding		Oily	
Hair	Brittle		Acne and rashes		Oily	
Teeth/Gums	Enamel issues/recession		Discoloration/tenderness		Excessive salivation	
Energy	Fluctuating - Hyper/Hypoactive		Exhaustion		Low and slow	
Sleep	Insomnia		Difficulty going to sleep		Frequent drowsiness	
Digestion	Constipation		Indigestion and loose stools		Mucous in stools	
Common issue	Neck pain		Middle back pain		Chest congestion	
Health conditions	Neck pain Low back and hip pain Early arthritis Colon or bone problems Nerve discorders		Middle back pain Joint inflammation Eye conditions and migraines Liver and gallbladder problems Cardiac conditions		Chest congestion Sinus conditions Fluid retention Weight gain	
In Stress	Fear, overwhelm, anxiety		Jealousy, criticism, anger		Greed, isolation, depression	
Totals	Vata		Pitta		Kapha	

Chakra Quiz

Answer for what feels most real most of the time. Total each Chakra area. For example, you will have a total for Root D, Root E, and Root B. If you have any imbalance, as in having more Ds and Es than Bs, refer to Chakra Basics to find Root Chakra techniques that support more balanced energy in this area.

Chakra Self-Study					
Deficient or excess is a generalization only. If you recognize yourself in a statement, as in "often" - put an "X in the box to the right.					
Chakra	**"D" - Deficient**		**"E" - Excess**		**"B" Balance**	
Root	My body is awkward.		My body slows me down.		My body is a safe place.	
Root	I don't want to belong.		I need others to know I'm ok.		Belonging is always possible.	
Root	Often lack boundaries.		Often rigid and aggressive.		I have boundaries and flexibility.	
Root	Big changes scare me.		Excitement helps me feel stable.		I feel content most of the time.	
Root	I don't need much.		I need more.		I have enough.	
Total	**Root Deficiency**		**Root Excess**		**Root Balance**	
Sacral	My body is rigid.		My body is compulsive.		My body is graceful.	
Sacral	I often deprive my own needs.		Manipulation helps fulfill my needs.		Meeting my needs is easy.	
Sacral	Desire scares me.		I need to feel attachment.		I am authentic in intimacy.	
Sacral	I feel out of place with strangers.		I like being the center of attention.		I give and receive openly.	
Sacral	I don't feel free.		I feel constant longing.		Life is pleasurable.	
Total	**Sacral Deficiency**		**Sacral Excess**		**Sacral Balance**	
Solar	It takes a while for action.		I am ready to compete.		I am reliable.	
Solar	I lack self-discipline.		I am often called stubborn.		My will is balanced.	
Solar	I feel weak/meek.		I am what I do.		I am powerful no matter what I do.	
Solar	I feel controlled by other's actions.		Control of others is often needed.		I do what's needed, mistakes are ok.	
Solar	Please tell me what to do.		I will not let you run my life.		I welcome insights into my decisions.	
Total	**Solar Deficiency**		**Solar Excess**		**Solar Balance**	
Heart	I have poor circulation.		My chest often feels tight.		My heart feels warm and free.	
Heart	Others can be intolerable.		I can be jealous and demanding.		Compassion prevails within me.	
Heart	I can't forgive myself.		I can't forgive others.		Forgiveness is given where needed.	
Heart	Lonely and critical.		Sacrificial caregiver.		I am often altruistic.	
Heart	I love you if you do _____.		I will entertain you until you love me.		My deep self-love is reflected in all.	
Total	**Heart Deficiency**		**Heart Excess**		**Heart Balance**	
Throat	I am shy.		I am a magnet for other's drama.		I am mindful in communication.	
Throat	My voice and rhythmn feel forced.		My voice and rhythmn are forceful.		My voice and body tunes in easily.	
Throat	I am an introvert.		I am the ringleader.		I listen and speak naturally.	
Throat	My voice doesn't usually matter.		I have an answer even if I don't know.		I listen and express true thoughts.	
Throat	Insecurity chatter.		Gossip chatter.		Objective truth.	
Total	**Throat Deficiency**		**Throat Excess**		**Throat Balance**	
3rd Eye	Poor vision.		Frequent head/eye conditions.		Clarity of vision and thought.	
3rd Eye	Poor memory.		Difficulty concentrating.		Good perceptions.	
3rd Eye	Difficulty seeing the future.		Delusional about the future.		6th sense.	
3rd Eye	Can't seem to get it down on paper.		Drawn to sleep aids to quiet my mind.		Visualization of concepts is easy.	
3rd Eye	There is only one way.		I am obsessed with figuring it out.		I trust my intuition.	
Total	**3rd Eye Deficiency**		**3rd Eye Excess**		**3rd Eye Balance**	
Crown	Migraines.		Confusion and dissassociation.		Awareness.	
Crown	Cynical about belief systems.		Thoughts of righteousness.		Wisdom.	
Crown	Apathetic about spirituality.		Spiritual additiction.		Spiritually connected.	
Crown	Holding tight to materials/greed.		Supporting extremist causes.		I objectively analyze and interpret.	
Crown	My beliefs are the only way.		I intellectualize superior to others.		The world is my teacher.	
Total	**Crown Deficiency**		**Crown Excess**		**Crown Balance**	

Subtle Energy Balancing

Dosha Basics

Vata

Overall.   Grounding, strength, and standing balances with moderation in flexibility.

Concerns.   Too much flexibility and instability, prone to injury & stiffness with age.

Examples.   Poses that are grounding, seated, slow and held for longer periods.

Basics.   Deepen breath first and warm up and exercise only to mild sweat.

Emphasize pelvis and colon (main sites of Vata).

Release tension in hips and lumbar spine but restrict amount of stretching.

Create stillness and strength in lower abdomen.

Twist only when breathing practice is good.

Backbend in grounded moderation.

Long and calm periods of rest.

Pitta

Overall.   Cooling, nurturing, expansive, relaxing, holds stands/balances.

Concerns.   Aggressive nature can mean technical proficiency at the expense of the spirit.

Examples.   Poses that are seated, slow Sun Salutations, Standing/Opening/Balancing, Shoulder Stand, Fish, Cobra, Bow, Forward Bends, Twists.

Basics.   Practice longer holds and cooling breath between efforting.

Revolved, seated twists and forward bends are cooling.

Emphasis calming of small intestine and liver (main sites of Pitta).

Headstands/handstands should not be practiced in warm body or room.

End practice feeling cool and relaxed.

Kapha

Overall.   Stimulating, faster, warming, energizing, releasing

Concerns.   Attempts to contort to "yogi" body results in limitations rather than wellness.

Examples.   Sun Salutation and Vinyasa (breath to movement), Jumping, Standing One-Legged open poses, Down Dog, Up Dog, Handstand, Bow, Camel, Locust, short Savasana

Basics.   Warm up gradually and practice to heavy sweat and heightened challenges.

Limit seated, forward bending, cooling, restorative and yin like poses.

Morning group classes promote most long-lasting benefits.

Add warming breathing techniques to sitting poses.

End practice feeling sharp and clear with emotional release.

Chakra Basics

Root/Security

Body Part.	Feet to Tailbone
Examples.	Easy Pose, Table, Table Circles, Side Gate, Lizard, Low Lunge, Child's Pose, Cobra.
Basics.	Stabilize and ground lower body.
	Breathing techniques with longer exhales.

Sacral/Feeling

Body Part.	Pelvis
Examples.	Cat/Cow, Cobra, Squat, Bridge, Spinal Series Low, Butterfly Knee Lift, Reverse Pigeon.
Basics.	Stable and fluid movement in sacral spine region.
	Breathing techniques that move breath fluidly through lower torso.

Solar Plexus/Action

Body Part.	Navel/Core
Examples.	Radiance Charger, Locust, Plank, Reverse Plank, Side Plank, Warriors, Breath of Fire.
Basics.	Strengthen lumbar region, overall core stabilization and posture, emphasize courage.
	Breathing techniques that fire up metabolism.

Heart/Compassion

Body Part.	Chest/Back
Examples.	Arm Swings, Shoulder Shrugs, Washing Machine, Camel, Wild Thing, Cannon breath.
Basics.	Back and chest movements that disperse stuck energy around the heart.
	Breathing techniques that dissipate heaviness in the chest.

Throat/Expression

Body Part.	Neck and Jaw
Examples.	Neck Circles, Head Nods, Sphynx, Fish, Lion's Breath, Whistle and Bumble Bee Breath.
Basics.	Move energy around the neck and cervical spine region.
	Breathing techniques that vibrate noises between the heart to throat.

3rd Eye/Vision

Body Part.	Forehead/Between Brows
Examples.	Down Dog, Puppy, Dolphin, Rabbit, Prasaritas, Skull Shining and Tattva Balance Breath.
Basics.	Lower the head below the heart.
	Breathing techniques that create lightness in the head (ex. Tattva Balance Breath)

Crown/Universal Connection

Body Part.	Top of Head
Examples.	Meditation, Legs Up the Wall, Mountain Brook, Savasana, Nadi Sushumna.
Basics.	Elevate, open and ground at the same time
	Use breathing techniques that emphasis equality of Nadis.

Vayu Basics

Prana Vayu

Direction.	Inward
Overall.	Inspiration to Move Forward
Examples.	Backbends
Basics.	Move energy toward the heart and head.
	Use breathing techniques with longer inhalations.

Apana Vayu

Direction.	Downward
Overall.	Stabilize and Eliminate
Examples.	Seated poses, folds
Basics.	Ground energy from pelvis to feet to promote release.
	Use breathing techniques with longer exhalations.

Samana Vayu

Direction.	Balancing
Overall.	Consolidating
Examples.	Balancing Poses, Sama Vritti
Basics.	Engage the core to support full body strength (ex. balancing poses).
	Use breathing techniques that center energy.

Udana Vayu

Direction.	Upward
Overall.	Elevating
Examples.	Inversions, Sat Kriya
Basics.	Move air towards neck.
	Use breathing techniques that push energy upward.

Vyana Vayu

Direction.	Expanding
Overall.	Circulating
Examples.	Sun Salutations, Ujjayi Breath
Basics.	Move energy through bodily systems.
	Use rhythmic breathing techniques.

Glossary